THE CAREER RESOURCE LIBRARY

Careers
in the
**Fashion
Industry**

John Giacobello

The Rosen Publishing Group, Inc.
NEW YORK

Dedicated to the legendary Don and Kelly

Published in 1999, 2003 by The Rosen Publishing Group, Inc.
29 East 21st Street, New York, NY 10010

Revised Edition 2003

Cover photo © Paul Barton/Corbis

Library of Congress Cataloging-in-Publication Data

Giacobello, John.
Careers in the fashion industry / by John Giacobello.
    p.   cm. — (Career resource library)
Includes bibliographical references and index.
Summary: Provides information about the educational requirements, employment opportunities, and creative potential within the world of fashion.
ISBN 0-8239-4082-9
1. Fashion—Vocational guidance—Juvenile literature. [1. Fashion—Vocational guidance. 2. Clothing trade—Vocational guidance. 3. Occupations. 4. Vocational guidance.] I. Title. II. Series: Career resource library (Rosen Publishing Group)
TT507.G48 1999
746.9'2'023—dc21   99-33843
                                                CIP

Manufactured in the United States of America

Contents

Your Place in the World of Fashion

Red lights flash and pulse. Throbbing dance music blares. Supermodel Naomi Campbell struts down a catwalk wearing a large, feathered headdress and a flowing ball gown, giving attitude to a celebrity-packed audience. MTV cameras are on one side, VH1 on the other. Joan Rivers gossips with Cindy Crawford backstage, while a frantic designer rushes to perfect his latest creation before it is paraded in front of the press. This is the world of fashion that we see regularly on television. But is this the real world of fashion?

Well, yes, it is. But it is only a small part of it. This is the part that the fashion industry likes to show the world because it generates publicity and excitement about fashion and helps to sell clothes. Many young people become interested in working in fashion because of the glamorous spectacle that has been presented to them through the media. But the real world of fashion is much more diverse, and it is filled with very real career opportunities—both in front of and away from the cameras and the spotlights. Not all opportunities are as exciting as the scene described here, but careers in fashion can be challenging, creative, and sometimes glamorous.

The Ups and Downs of Fashion

The world of fashion provides excellent creative careers for artistic people, but there are plenty of business-oriented positions available as well. This duality helps make the fashion world interesting, especially since crossover between different types of jobs is always possible within the field. Many fashion jobs offer great potential for fun, enormous salaries, and international travel. There is also potential for quiet, solitude, and security for those seeking such things in a job, depending upon which end of the business they go into.

The downside is that fashion moves in cycles, and what goes up must come down. Many who work in the industry describe it as fickle. Fashion is known for the eccentric, creative people it attracts, and these people can sometimes be difficult to work with (and for). At their worst, people in the fashion industry can be brutal and backstabbing, but every business has its ugly side.

The working environment of some fashion jobs is less than inspiring. Even the highest-paid designers spend most of their time working in a small space, surrounded by piles of fabric, noisy cutters, and the hum of sewing machines. Most fashion jobs involve long and labor-intensive hours, and starting salaries are generally low. Many of those who work in the industry say that you have to really love fashion to put up with its risks and pitfalls.

Is a Fashion Career for Me?

If you think that you might like to be a part of the fashion world, you should first take a good look at your personality. Analyze your likes, dislikes, and interests. Get started by making a list of your accomplishments. Try writing down all of the things that you feel have shaped who you are, any life experiences from which you have learned, and anything that you are proud to have achieved. It does not matter if these things are directly related to fashion or not.

Now look over your list of accomplishments and achievements. What do they say about who you are? What are your strong points? For example, getting all A's on your finals shows an ability to deal with pressure, an important trait in the fashion world. Directing or performing in your school's production of a play or a talent show indicates creativity and a theatrical instinct, traits that are valuable to the fashion designer or photographer. Working as a part-time cashier for a department store shows initiative, responsibility, and some knowledge of clothing and fashion. Start thinking about how your accomplishments reflect who you are and how they might be applied to a career.

What do you do for fun? If you participate in sports, this might indicate that you work well on a team and know how to handle competitive situations. Do you enjoy reading fashion magazines or watching fashion shows on television? Do you enjoy getting dressed up and looking your best? Do you feel at ease socializing at parties or functions? All of these things can come into play in a fashion career. What you like to do in your spare time says a lot about you and, possibly, about your future.

Even if you know that you want to work in fashion, you may not be sure exactly which fashion career path is right for you. First, it might be a good idea to figure out what you are looking for in a job and make a list of those qualities. For example, would you rather have clearly defined responsibilities or the freedom to shape your own job? Do you like to work alone or on a team? Would you prefer to work nine to five or to have an unpredictable schedule? Would you like to travel? Where would you like to live? Do you work well under pressure? Ask yourself these questions and any others you can think of concerning your future occupation. Then, as you go through this book, look for the career choices that best match the description you have created.

When considering career choices, it is important that you know yourself. You need to realize that who you are keeps changing, so it is important to spend time updating your lists and exploring different possibilities as you grow and evolve as a person. Deciding on a career path is one of the most important decisions of your life—one that requires constant reevaluation. Understanding what you want, what you are good at, and where your weaknesses lie will also help you to put your best foot forward in a job interview. Employers can sense uncertainty, and the questions you are asked during the interview may reveal things about yourself that even you were not aware of!

Learning your strengths and weaknesses is not as difficult as it may seem. Everybody has weak points, not just you. Everybody also has strengths. You just have to be open to realizing and developing the strong points. Try not to compare yourself too harshly with others; there will always be someone out there who is better at something than you are. That can quickly become discouraging in an industry as competitive as fashion. Focus on what you do well and how you can use it to your advantage in following your career path. And with hard work, any weakness can eventually become a strength.

You can work in fashion whether you are male or female. There are no insurmountable gender boundaries, although more than 80 percent of all workers in the fashion industry are women. This varies from job to job, however. For example, most apparel and window display designers are men. And as with any career, there are always individual cases of sexism and other types of discrimination. But there is no fashion career that completely excludes women or men.

Fashion Past and Future

The business of manufacturing clothing in the United States began with the Industrial Revolution in the early nineteenth century, which is when textile machines and power looms came into widespread use in the United States. Before that time, most families in America made their own clothes. Only the wealthy could afford to have clothing made for them. After the invention of the cotton gin in 1793, people who operated small mills began to sell fabric to housewives. Soon women in different parts of the United States were sewing clothes by hand and selling them to local American workers.

By the 1860s, paper patterns for clothing were being sold. The sewing machine made possible the development of the garment industry, and America's growing middle class welcomed the idea of purchasing ready-made clothing rather than making their own.

Careers in the Fashion Industry

By the beginning of the twentieth century, the apparel industry in the United States was growing rapidly. Large clothing factories sprang up in New York and New England, and the Lower East Side of New York City developed into the center of U.S. fashion manufacturing. New York set the clothing standard for the entire country, and buyers (people who purchase clothing for department stores) flocked there to place orders for the latest collections.

Over time, fashion became somewhat more accessible to the middle class rather than just to the elite, wealthy few who had enjoyed it in the past. It became part of mainstream culture, something that everyday people began to read about and discuss with great excitement. People from all walks of life enjoyed fashion magazines and advertising.

But generally, it was still only the members of high society who could actually afford original designs. The lavish dances and parties held by the rich were like fashion shows where designers could always count on receiving publicity and exposure for their clothing. Many of these designs were then knocked off (copied and mass-produced) and sold at more affordable prices. In this way, the middle class became directly involved with fashion beyond merely reading about it in magazines and in the society pages. Knockoffs became a fashion tradition that persists despite the objections of most designers.

Though the business of manufacturing affordable clothing grew quite rapidly, this did not stop some women from sewing clothes for themselves and their families. Many popular fashion magazines included patterns so that their readers could create the designs they had just read about. A significant number of people desired handmade clothes and were rich enough to pay others to make them. The most exclusive dressmakers accepted commissions to make clothing for wealthy families, and they eventually opened their own shops.

Even before the development of the fashion industry in the United States, Paris had established itself as a fashion center. During the eighteenth century, a French dressmaker became one of the first in her trade to attain individual fame. Rose Bertin was the full-time dressmaker for Queen Marie Antoinette, who was known for the splendor and extravagance of her wardrobe.

In the years following the French Revolution, which began in 1789, elaborate fashion went out of style to be replaced by a more "democratic" look, which meant the look of the more common person. The next dressmaker to influence French society did not emerge until 1858. His name was Charles Frederick Worth, and he designed clothing for the empress Eugénie. Worth was an unusual figure in the French fashion world for two reasons—he was a man, and he was English.

Worth is often credited with setting many of the standards used by fashion designers today. He was the first dressmaker to create entire collections as opposed to individual pieces, the first to show his work on live models, and the first to have his own salon. Worth did not go to his clients; his clients came to him—a new approach that reflected the growing importance of designers.

American and French designers have always competed against one another. Most often the French have been the leaders, with many American designers taking inspiration from—or simply copying—Parisian designs.

Exceptions occurred during World War I (1914 to 1918) and World War II (1939 to 1945), when the German occupation of French soil disrupted France's fashion industry. During these periods, American designers moved to the forefront, becoming more creative and self-reliant. After the wars, Paris resumed its role as the fashion leader.

This fashion tug-of-war continued until the early 1960s, when the young people of "swinging" London inspired British designers. The "youthquake" movement was all about the style, creativity, and energy of the young. Fashion became antiestablishment (against the average public image of fashion), with new British designers such as Mary Quant and Zandra Rhodes leading the way. Naturally, Paris and New York followed suit with their own youth-oriented contributions. Although Paris maintained its dominance in the world fashion market, Italian and Spanish designers also became increasingly important. In the 1970s, Japanese fashion skyrocketed in popularity and importance.

Today many American designers are acclaimed for their contributions to the international fashion scene, particularly in sportswear and casual wear. New York City is still an important fashion center, along with Los Angeles, Miami, Dallas, Chicago, and Atlanta. All of these cities have a fashion district, which is a specific area of the city where most of the fashion manufacturers are located. In New York City, the fashion district runs along Broadway and Seventh Avenue, between 34th and 41st streets.

Fashion has changed a great deal since the mid-twentieth century, transforming itself as society has changed. Before the 1960s, the rules of fashion could be strict; those who found themselves out of style were generally excluded or ridiculed. But the rules loosened as women's roles and needs changed. Today most designers, manufacturers, fashion magazines, and advertisers try to give people ideas and options, not dictate rules.

Today American women—and men—do not like having fashion standards dictated to them. Many women pride themselves on developing their own sense of individual style. Today's women usually do not look to fashion magazines and television shows to be told exactly what they must wear. Instead they want suggestions on how they can cultivate their own style. People generally understand that the metal-and-plastic gown clinking and squeaking down the runway is intended for media attention and special occasions, not for everyday wear to the office or grocery store. Anyone working in fashion must understand the savvy consumer of today and be able to anticipate changes in the culture that will affect what people wear and how they wear it.

Creative Careers: Design

2

Donna had been interested in clothing since she was a child. She loved looking in her parents' closet at all the different colors and textures of the fabrics that hung there. As she got older, she began reading fashion magazines and did a bit of acting in her high school's drama department. She studied the similarities between the costumes she wore for plays and the clothes she wore every day. She taught herself to sew and was able to repair torn costumes backstage. She even learned to do alterations when something did not fit an actor or actress properly.

Donna decided that she wanted to go to fashion school and become a fashion designer. She knew that she was good with clothing, and she wanted a glamorous career. But she was not sure if that was what fashion design was really all about. Donna wondered how many designers work without huge salaries and recognition. She became confused because she was not sure if she was interested in design for the actual work involved or for the glamour and excitement that she thought would come with it.

Fashion Design

The career of fashion design is probably one of the first jobs people think of when they try to imagine a career in fashion. One reason may be that as fashion becomes more popular in mainstream American media, designers are becoming celebrities. MTV's *House of Style* featured "Todd Time," a popular segment hosted by designer Todd Oldham. A documentary called *Unzipped*, about the well-known and eccentric designer Isaac Mizrahi, was well received by both critics and the public. And the death of the great Italian designer Gianni Versace, who was shot and killed outside his Miami home in 1997, became front-page news around the world.

But what is the real world of fashion design all about? The truth is that only a small handful of designers ever become famous. Most designers and assistant designers work behind the scenes for salaries that range from extremely high to unbelievably low. Someone entering the world of fashion design should not necessarily assume that he or she will become as rich and famous as Vera Wang, who designs for celebrities like Vanessa Williams and Sharon Stone. But nobody should rule out that level of success either, because it could happen!

So what exactly does a clothing designer do, besides taking that bow at the end of the runway show and hugging the exhausted models? Although a designer may wear many hats and perform a variety of tasks, from sewing to sketching to schmoozing at parties, fashion design is an art form that is all about generating ideas. There are no clearly defined duties or hours for this position. Responsibilities may vary tremendously depending upon which apparel manufacturer or store a designer works for. A designer may also be self-employed and work for specific clients. Designing clothing is definitely not a career for a person who longs for a nine-to-five schedule and a secure, stable income.

Clothing designers must always, no matter who they work for, take the first step in the long process of turning an idea into a product. That first step is the creation of the idea itself. Designers may achieve this alone or as part of a team.

Generally designers are expected to create a line of clothing for a particular season. The line is usually developed and conveyed using a series of sketches, which the designer must produce. A designer may choose different methods of working out his or her ideas, such as draping fabric on a mannequin or testing out colors and textures using computer software. A line usually includes variations on a specific theme or several unified themes and should be created about two seasons ahead of time.

A fashion designer should possess excellent management skills, since designers often have to supervise entire teams of assistants, sample makers, and pattern cutters. The input and assistance of others is essential to bring an idea to life, but most designers try to be involved in each step of the process so that their original concept is not lost along the way.

Designers also do a great deal of shopping, sometimes to research other people's designs and sometimes to buy fabrics. They spend time at American and

European showrooms, mills, fabric fairs, and sometimes thrift shops and flea markets, searching for just the right texture and color of fabric. Some advantages to designing include discounts on clothing and fabric as well as free admission to fabulous fashion shows, parties, and fund-raisers. Successful designers get to rub elbows with just about everyone who's anyone!

Designers usually specialize in either men's or women's clothing. Most prefer to design for women, for both creative and economic reasons. Creatively, women's clothing offers more color, glamour, and variety than men's apparel. And economically, women's fashions change more often than men's do, so there is generally more money to be made in designing women's clothes. But many designers of menswear, such as Giorgio Armani and Calvin Klein, have managed to be extremely successful and sometimes even adventurous with men's clothing while maintaining the reputation for good taste upon which they have built their reputations. Some young designers move toward menswear because the competition is not quite as fierce as it can be in women's apparel.

Designers usually live in the cities where most fashion is produced. In the United States, those areas are New York City, Los Angeles, Dallas, and Chicago. Some other cities specialize in certain kinds of clothing. For example, Denver is known for producing skiwear. Boston is a center for coats and bridal wear. Miami focuses on swimwear and children's wear, and Philadelphia produces a great deal of sportswear and outerwear.

If you think a career in fashion design might interest you, try to take any art and drawing classes that are available in your school. Also, if your school offers sewing and home economics, be sure to take those classes as well. You may be able to get involved with relevant extracurricular activities such as drawing or a sewing club. Also, it is extremely helpful to know how to use a computer. An excellent part-time job would be working as a salesperson at a clothing store. This would help you learn firsthand what people are looking for in an outfit or article of clothing.

Another good habit for fashion students is collecting photos from fashion magazines and keeping them in photo albums or scrapbooks. You can get a head start on this now, and it may become an enjoyable and affordable hobby. Find photographs that inspire you. Do not limit yourself to *Vogue* and *Harper's Bazaar*, although these are both excellent sources. Look for still photographs from movies, concerts, and the theater. Find copies of works of art that you enjoy. Even advertising offers some fascinating images. All of these things can help you define your sense of style and figure out what kind of designer you might like to be someday.

Anyone who has good ideas, along with the skill and nerve to express and promote them, has the potential to make it in fashion design. There are no educational requirements for this career, and in fact many successful designers today have had no formal training. However, being educated in certain areas can make it easier to express your ideas clearly and may give you an edge over the competition. Seventy-five percent of the leading fashion designers in New York City attended a design school, and many fashion schools have excellent programs and resources to help you find a job after graduation.

Drawing is one of the most common ways for a designer to convey ideas, so classes in sketching and drawing are extremely valuable. Many colleges and fashion schools also include courses in their curriculum such as draping, pattern making, merchandising, and textiles. Art history is also an important subject for a young designer to study for examples and inspiration; basic anatomy can give you a good sense of how the body works and how clothing should fit. A designer also needs to know how to sew and should be able to cut patterns from muslin. Muslin is an inexpensive fabric that designers use to test patterns before attempting to cut them with more expensive fabric. All of these skills are generally taught as part of the standard curriculum at most design schools.

Some requirements for this career cannot be taught in school, like a natural flair for and love of fashion. A good eye for color is also essential, and a patient, determined personality can be indispensable for dealing with the rough times, difficult people, and dry spells common in the profession.

If you are interested in going to fashion school, you may find your choices of places to live somewhat limited. The best fashion schools in the country are located in cities that are considered the fashion capitals: New York, Los Angeles, and Chicago. These are large cities that many people consider exciting and stimulating places to live, but they are not for everyone. Some find them overcrowded and hectic. In New York, Parsons School of Design and the Fashion Institute of Technology offer majors in fashion design as well as many other fashion-related careers. In Los Angeles, the Otis College of Art and Design offers a four-year program in fine arts and fashion design, and it is conveniently located in the heart of downtown L.A.'s garment district. Chicago has the Illinois Institute of Art and the International Academy of Merchandising and Design, both of which offer degrees in fashion design.

Careers in the Fashion Industry

Studying fashion abroad is another fascinating option. The London College of Fashion offers excellent workrooms, design studios, and a fashion theater with a permanent catwalk. The Paris Fashion Institute's Web site describes it as "a virtual living textbook of fashion creation, history, and marketing." In Canada, Montreal Superior Fashion School offers a degree program in fashion management and design with three different options: fashion styling and design, fashion merchandising, and fashion industrial management.

Usually a designer starts out as an assistant designer or as an apprentice to a designer. This is a give-and-take relationship that a young, aspiring designer enters into with a more established designer. The apprentice assists the designer with anything the designer might need. This could include delivering packages, sewing, or shopping for fabric and supplies. Many assistant designers shop for trim (such as ribbon and buttons), sketch ideas, and conduct research at museums and libraries.

In return the apprentice learns about fashion design up close and gains experience of immeasurable value to his or her career. Pay is usually extremely low in this position since it is more an opportunity to gain experience than to make money. Unfortunately, most careers in fashion do start out on the low end of the salary scale, but the industry provides much growth opportunity for those who are talented and willing to work hard.

Average salaries in fashion design are hard to gauge because of their wide variation. Interns may work for free, whereas assistant designers may make anywhere from $15,000 to $30,000 to start. From there, salary possibilities for established designers are limitless.

Some make comfortable livings, from $40,000 to $60,000, whereas others skyrocket into the millions.

To find a job as an assistant designer, it is essential to have a portfolio. This is a book you put together and carry with you as often as possible that contains your ideas, usually in sketch form. The portfolio should also include your résumé, which explains in detail any fashion experience you have. Even your part-time job folding sweaters at the Gap or your brief stint fetching coffee for Donna Karan's accountant's receptionist should be included on this résumé. Just the fact that you have any kind of experience related to fashion shows some initiative.

The résumé should also detail your education. Fashion courses are especially impressive, and you should take this opportunity to list projects and show sketches. The drawings should be on clean, high-quality paper and should showcase your ideas in sportswear, coats, suits, and evening wear. Remember to attach fabric swatches to show what types and colors of fabrics you envision with the designs you have sketched.

Employers will also expect to see a special kind of sketch in your portfolio called a flat. A flat can be described as a blueprint for your designs. It shows in detail how a garment would be constructed, laid out front and back, whereas the other sketches aim to give an impression of how the outfit would look when worn by a model. Clothing producers work from flats when constructing a garment from a design.

You should have as many sketches and flats as possible so that you can gear your portfolio toward the specific company or designer you are showing it to. For example, you should have enough sketches of suits available to assemble your portfolio for an interview with a suit manufacturer. Or you may need to have a good mix of coats and evening wear for a certain department store. Always research the company or individual you will be interviewing with.

What It's Like: An Interview with a Fashion Design Student

Don, a student at the Fashion Institute of Technology (FIT) in New York City, is pursuing a career in fashion design. He has always been fascinated by clothing and decided when he was twenty years old that he wanted to be a designer. In New York, he enjoys going out to big nightclubs to see all the interesting styles and outrageous outfits. He has been attending FIT for three years and has taken courses in sewing, pattern making, draping, and different types of drawing. He works full-time at a technology company to put himself through school.

What made you decide you wanted to be a fashion designer?
I have a passion for creating clothes. It is what I understand; it just makes sense to me.

What do you like most about going to fashion school?
I love learning the craft of fashion design. It is very satisfying to finally learn how to take the things that I see in my head and make them real, to get them out in some form.

What do you like least about school?

Mainly that I just don't have enough time to devote to it. It is hard to work full-time, go to school, do homework, and relax. I wish I had gone to fashion school instead of college, where I majored in accounting. If I'd had more faith in my ability and my parents had been more supportive, I would have gone back then. But it took a long time for me to realize that I could actually do it if I tried. It really helped to go out to nightclubs. That gave me the opportunity to see a lot of different creations and to play with my own outfits.

Which of the classes that you have taken at FIT did you like the least?

I didn't really enjoy pattern making because the professor was dull. It was also difficult to carry all those supplies back and forth to class, and the work was extremely meticulous. Everything has to be very exact. There are so many steps, and learning to make patterns takes such a long time.

Which of the classes did you like the most?

I really liked draping. The professor was excellent and knew how to inspire the class. He was tough, but he gave us a lot of useful information about the fashion industry. He was also very realistic and was interested in helping us to develop our creativity, unlike many other teachers I've had.

How is fashion school different from the way you thought it would be?

There is a lot more art involved than I realized. In general, it is more difficult than I thought it would be and much more time-consuming. Before I started school, I felt as though I had a lot of ideas. Soon I realized I had only two. It takes a while to gain confidence in what you're doing, and that's what really helps to get ideas flowing.

Is there any advice you would give a young person who is thinking about going to fashion school?

Don't do it—I don't need any younger competition! [Laughs.] No, actually I would say you need to realize ahead of time that fashion school is not really glamorous. Don't do it because you think it's going to be all fun. Doing well takes a lot of hard work. Also, you should study as much fashion history as possible and learn about what's happened in the industry beyond the last two years. Finally, it is very important to have a passion for what you're doing. You have to really want it in order to stick with it.

What fashion magazines do you think young people getting into the industry should read every month?

The American magazines *Vogue* and *Harper's Bazaar* are definitely the most important ones for keeping abreast of what's going on, but foreign magazines like Italian *Vogue* and *The Face* are usually better and more interesting. They tend to take more risks. It's important to get a lot of different perspectives.

What do you plan to do with your schooling?

I hope to get an assistant design position at a small design house and then to one day have my own company. I want to get all the technical information I can from school, like the basics of how to draw and sew. But I also want to learn as much as I can about how the industry works before throwing myself into it.

Specialty and Theatrical Apparel Design

Cynthia loved designing clothes. She graduated from Parsons School of Design in New York and soon landed an assistant design position at Todd Oldham. She thought she had everything she wanted, but something was missing. She was growing tired of the fashion world's fickleness and constant cycles. Cynthia had the feeling that this career path might not be right for her. She still wanted to design clothes, but she wished she had some other options.

There are some interesting fashion design careers that lie off the beaten path of standard evening and day wear and that require a great deal of specialized knowledge. Someone has to design the sparkling costumes for the lavish Broadway musical or the authentically groovy outfits for the period film set in the 1970s. What about the slick Lycra shorts that seem to fit runners like a second skin and allow total freedom of movement? Or the stunning bridal gown, or the impeccably tailored soldier's uniform? Well-designed, specialized clothing is essential to people in all kinds of professions and lifestyles. Designing clothing for theater or film, athletics, or for the military constitutes a vital contribution.

Costume Design

If you combine an interest in the performing arts with a flair for fashion, costume design may be a career worth exploring. Most people who design costumes consider it a true labor of love, where they can be a part of the worlds of music, opera, dance, or theater by using their own unique talents.

One of the major differences between designing costumes and designing everyday apparel is that costume designers work with unusual fabrics and create styles that span the centuries and beyond. There is no limit to the imaginations of those who combine their creative efforts to put together a theatrical production, and this kind of no-holds-barred freedom is exactly what appeals most to many costume designers.

Of course, there are some limitations. The costume designer must work closely with the director to interpret the production and determine how his or her designs can convey the necessary information to the audience. This information can include the time period and setting of the production, the background and personality traits of the characters, events taking place at certain moments in the production, and countless other subtle messages. Fashion conveys similar messages in our day-to-day lives, to the extent that some people would argue that everything we wear throughout our lives is nothing more than costume. What we wear may seem normal to us at this point in time, but someday costume designers will be conducting research about how to outfit productions set at the beginning of the twenty-first century!

As a costume designer, you spend much of your time brainstorming and sketching ideas in your studio. Creating and cutting out a pattern for the garment is the next step, followed by scouring the city for fabrics that suit your creation. Fabric stores, thrift shops, and flea markets will likely become your regular hangouts. You will probably construct the costumes and do all of the sewing and alterations as well, unless you become an established, extremely successful designer who can hire people to do the sewing. Costumes must be eye-catching and accurate and as durable as possible, to endure night after night of performance and rehearsal. As a costume designer, you will also be expected to attend rehearsals, much like the actors and actresses in the production.

If you know how to design and sew, the best way to gain experience in costume design is by getting in touch with small, local theater or dance groups and offering to design free costumes for a show. High school productions can provide excellent hands-on experience as well. Working on these types of shows can give you a pretty good idea of what the profession is like and help you determine your true feelings about this career.

Careers in the Fashion Industry

If you are in high school, take as many sewing classes as possible. You will need strong sewing skills even to work on a small production in your town or city. Drawing is also important, so pay close attention in art class. Your first instruction in other skills, such as pattern making, fabrics, and clothing construction, may have to come from books unless you can find a class in costume making. If you have any interest in acting, directing, or working with scenery and lights, try to get involved with your high school drama club. This can provide you with an important edge in costume design by getting you well acquainted with the world of theater. And, of course, go to as many plays and movies as possible, paying close attention to the costumes and their construction.

Educational requirements for a costume designer are similar to those for a fashion designer. There are no specific requirements, but a college or design school degree in fashion design can certainly give you an edge over the competition. There are also apprenticeships available with many theater groups. Some colleges have prestigious theater departments, which are excellent places for fledgling costume designers to take their first steps.

Opportunities for costume designers lie primarily in film, dance, and theater, although some of them design for costume shops and seasonal Halloween stores. There are not quite as many jobs available in costume design as there are in standard apparel design, and the average pay is somewhat lower, so the best reason to go into this career is love for the work. The starting salary ranges from $13,000 to $18,000 yearly but with experience can go above $40,000. Some costume designers become extremely famous and make a great deal of money, such as the legendary movie studio designer Edith Head, but these cases are rare.

Dance, Exercise, and Sports Design

Some clothing designers choose to create apparel for dance and exercise. Often these types of clothing serve similar purposes in that they must be comfortable, keep muscles warm, and absorb perspiration. The fabrics most often used are cotton and Lycra—usually a blend of the two. Designing shoes for dance and exercise is an especially complex skill since there is so much legwork involved in both activities, and extensive knowledge of the foot's anatomy is essential. A designer of dance and exercise clothing must understand both the human body and the kinds of movements and strains involved in these disciplines. Employment opportunities for these types of designers include working for large companies, such as Kling's Motion Unlimited and Leo's, or even starting a business.

Designers with strong sports backgrounds may go into designing for professional athletes. Most specialize in one particular sport, from figure skating to football, and learn all there is to know about it. This kind of extensive knowledge is required to be successful in this career because the needs of each athlete are so specific. The cut of a pair of baseball pants or tennis shorts could have a major effect on an athlete's ability to perform at his or her best.

Sports is not the best field for designers who are aiming to open their own businesses. The only real opportunities are designing team uniforms and practice gear for large manufacturers and outlet stores. Because sports and fashion are unusual backgrounds for one person to combine, there are numerous opportunities in this field for people with this rare combination of skills. An ability to communicate with athletes and coaches is essential, and the clothes you design must help athletes to perform well and look good doing it.

Special-Occasion Apparel Design

So what exactly qualifies as a special occasion in fashion, besides the September issue of *Vogue* finally hitting the newsstands? Well, a wedding is pretty important, and wedding gowns require a special kind of design. Some other special occasions include religious events and graduations.

Many designers work only with bridal gowns. Because the bridal industry is such an enormous and important business, bridal designers are never short on customers. Some work in the bridal departments of department stores, whereas others design for boutiques specializing in wedding attire.

Bridal designers must keep up-to-date with mainstream fashion, since these cycles do affect their industry. They must also be skilled at creating works that are tastefully unique and sometimes slightly unusual without going too far. Most women want to buy something eye-catching and interesting for such an important event in their lives while staying within certain traditional guidelines.

Prepare for this career the same way you would for a career in any other type of clothing design, but be sure to devour as many bridal magazines as possible. Analyze the photos and read the articles to become familiar with the words and phrases associated with this highly specialized field. Spend some time thinking about the importance and meaning behind what you would be doing and the sacred role that marriage plays in so many lives. If you know how to sew, experiment with delicate fabrics like silk, satin, and lace.

The best way to get started designing bridal gowns is to apply for a job as a seamstress or assistant designer with a bridal shop or department store and learn as much as possible while working toward a promotion to designer. Average salaries for this career range from $20,000 to $50,000, and top designers can earn up to $100,000.

Designing uniforms is another career that few people think of when considering fashion opportunities. This may be because it is not the most creative or glamorous design job, but uniform design can be a much more stable career than other types of clothing design. To be a successful uniform designer, you need to become expert at putting new and unique spins on traditional designs. Most of the jobs available are with large firms, where you would sketch ideas and sew together apparel for mail carriers, soldiers, police officers, and others.

Accessory Design

As a young girl, Sheila was amazed at how many little pieces of clothing and jewelry her parents would put on when they got ready to go out. Her mother usually wore high-heeled shoes, a scarf tied around her head, earrings, a necklace, rings on her fingers, a bracelet, a watch, glasses with designer frames, and a pretty pin on her lapel. Her father did not wear as many items, but there was almost always a gold watch, black shoes, a tie and tie clasp, gloves, and a belt with a shiny gold buckle. She could not believe how much clothing a person could wear at one time!

As she got older, Sheila enjoyed buying her own accessories as well as giving and receiving them as gifts. She wondered who made the beautiful jewelry, shoes, and other small clothing items that she cherished. She also wondered if other people saw them the way she did, as little works of art that you could carry with you and display all the time and sometimes as sentimental items that held special meaning. She thought about how wonderful it would be to make a living by creating such things for other people to enjoy.

Some people looking into different fashion careers may consider the area of accessory design limiting at first. But designing accessories includes much more than just creating jewelry. Other accessories include hats, gloves, shoes, eyewear, scarves, ties, belts, and buttons. These essential items can make or break an outfit, and there is a whole world of career options available for the right people.

Like clothing design, accessory design is separated into accessories for women and men. Also like clothing design, most designers would rather go into women's accessories because women accessorize more than men. Learning to design just about any kind of accessory requires training, whether it is through school or on the job. Some accessories require more extensive training than others.

Jewelry design is fairly complex and extremely meticulous. People may design jewelry for women, men, or both, including rings, necklaces, bracelets, and earrings. Most jewelry designers both design and create the piece, so it is important for someone going into this career to be very good with his or her hands. Patience, coordination, and a strong fashion sense are necessary traits for a jewelry designer. These artists use many different stones, metals, tools, and chemicals to work their magic, and the skills take years to develop. Sometimes computers are used to aid in the design process.

Someone skilled at jewelry design could also become a jeweler. Jewelers must be skilled at jewelry sales, buying, repair, design, cutting, and appraisal. However, most specialize in one or more of these areas. Many start out as clerks in jewelry stores and learn their skills on the job. They may also work for specialized jewelry repair shops.

A jeweler who owns a shop becomes involved in all aspects of running a business, such as personnel, marketing, and accounting. There are about 30,000 jewelers in the United States, and about 35 percent of these are self-employed.

Designing hats is a profession known as millinery. Millinery and shoemaking are extremely specialized skills, since creating clothing perfectly suited to the head and foot requires knowledge and understanding of human anatomy. There are about 22,000 shoe and leather workers in this country, and about 4,000 of those workers own shops.

Designing neckties for men is a less complicated procedure. Even so, it requires certain skills, such as thread dyeing, pattern and color matching, and working with silks and other fabrics. An understanding of men's fashion is also important. Ties are often worn in a business setting, and many men take them very seriously as a way to make a first impression. Belt, wallet, and briefcase design involve a great deal of leather working and can also be creative and rewarding career options. Designing frames for sunglasses and eyeglasses is another highly specialized career with tremendous potential.

If you are in high school and think that you might have a knack for designing accessories, take as many art classes as you possibly can. Read fashion magazines and pay close attention to articles written about accessories and the use of accessories in fashion layouts. Television shows like CNN's *Style* and VH1's *Fashion File* often feature stories about the hot accessory designers of the moment. Often the designers will talk about how they got started in the field and what inspires them. You should also be able to find information at the library. If jewelry design interests you, you can use just about anything around the house to start experimenting, from old beads to pins and paper clips. Have fun and be creative with whatever you can find!

Further education for this field is not a requirement, but it can be extremely helpful. If you attend fashion school or college, you may be able to major in accessory design or even more specific areas such as jewelry design or millinery. If these majors are not available, classes in metalworking, fashion design, textiles, sketching, computers, and crafts can give you the background that you will need. Most of what you learn about accessory design will come from an experienced designer rather than classes, so you will eventually need to look for a craftsperson to apprentice with. While apprenticing, you will learn and practice your craft until you become skilled enough to produce items that can be sold to clients and store owners or be able to sell your ideas to manufacturing firms.

The job prospects for accessory design are excellent because accessories are always in demand. But this does not mean that finding a job in this field will be easy. You can work for an accessory store, a department store, or an accessory-manufacturing firm. These positions can be found in the want ads of your local newspaper or through a design school's job placement center. If you decide to go the self-employed route, you will need to work extremely hard to pitch your line to department stores and boutiques. You must also keep your products fresh and interesting in order to attract new customers and keep the old ones excited about your work.

The average American accessory designer earns about $600 per week, although yearly earnings can fluctuate from $10,000 to several million dollars per year depending on the success of the designs. Success is a combination of hard work, talent, networking, and a large dose of luck. The power of being at the right place at the right time cannot be underestimated, and after a while many people learn where the right places are.

Textile Technology

Fabric is a booming industry in itself and a high-tech one at that. After all, fabric is literally the stuff from which fashion is made. Much work goes into creating and selling textiles, and there are many career opportunities in this field. Such jobs range from technical problem solving to product development and quality assurance. You can read about many of these options at the library if you are interested. In this book, we will touch on textile design, textile engineering, textile management and technology, and textile chemistry.

Textile Design

Although it is one of the lesser-known positions in the fashion industry, textile design is extremely important. Without all of the creative minds and skilled hands that are constantly working to make new and interesting fabrics, there would be no beautiful creations on runways, in clothing stores, or on the street. Fabrics can truly inspire designers. They play a major role in turning clothing ideas into real products and sometimes into haute couture (high fashion) works of art.

Because there is always a large demand for fabric designers, the job outlook is extremely favorable. The textile industry has become very sophisticated in the past twenty years, and the technology continues to advance to meet the changing needs of the fashion industry.

A career in textile design requires skill in sewing, knitting, dyeing materials, and weaving. These are skills that you can learn and develop in fashion school, and there are no educational requirements for the position so long as you possess the necessary skills. You can get started as early as high school by taking sewing courses through your home economics department. It is important to learn as much as possible about fibers and textiles if you are interested in this career. You will also need to have a good sense of colors and how they work together. Strong computer skills are essential as well.

Fabric designers generally work either for manufacturing firms or their own companies. Entry-level salaries for this position generally range from $250 to $350 per week. Experienced fabric designers can make $50,000 to $100,000 a year.

Textile Engineering

If you are interested in fashion and your strongest subjects in school are science and math, textile engineering may be for you. Although textile design, as previously described, is still an important part of the fashion industry, the creation of fabrics becomes a more highly specialized and complicated task as technology advances. Large companies are constantly searching for new ways to mass-produce textiles efficiently. Textile engineering probes deeply into the chemical structure and properties of fabrics and the fibers from which they are made. It is a less creative and more strictly scientific career than textile design.

The starting salary range for a career in textile engineering is generally between $28,000 and $40,000 per year. A college degree is required, and the coursework focuses on mechanical, electrical, industrial, and chemical engineering.

Textile Chemistry

Textile chemistry is an extremely specialized field. It includes careers in textile dyeing and finishing, technical services, product development, polymer science, and environmental control. Textile chemistry focuses on the physics and chemistry of the polymers (chemical compounds) that form the fibers in textiles. Those interested in this field must be strong in science, chemistry, and math. Starting salaries range from $35,000 to $43,000.

Putting Your Best Face Forward: Modeling and Makeup

3

"Oh, you are so pretty—you should definitely model." Tina heard these words all the time. She tried not to let it go to her head, but she did sometimes wonder if she had a chance as a model. Tina was only sixteen, but she was tall and slender with impeccable bone structure and good skin.

The idea of modeling was very exciting, but Tina was a very practical girl, and she did not intend to rush into anything blindly. She had a lot of questions that she wanted answered first, like how tall do you have to be to model? Is it really enough just to be pretty by your friends' and family's standards, or is it a whole other ball game in the fashion world? Where does a model have to live? How do you get started? How long does a good modeling career last? Tina intended to find out the answers to these and all of her other questions before

*thinking seriously about a modeling career.
After that, who knew?*

Modeling

Modeling is one of the best-known careers in fashion and also one of the most hungrily sought after. Many young women and men dream of striking glamorous poses in fabulous designer ensembles, as flashbulbs go off and huge sums of money roll into their bank accounts. As with most fashion careers, this type of success is certainly possible. But in modeling there is almost always a great deal of struggle and failure that comes first, and often that long-awaited success never even arrives. Even when success does happen, modeling is not the easy job many people believe it to be. It can be exhausting physically, mentally, and emotionally.

This is not meant to discourage anyone from trying to break into modeling. It is important to have a realistic picture of how difficult and cruel the modeling universe can be. The pressure is often tremendous, and anyone not prepared for rejection and frustration can be absolutely crushed before he or she really gets started.

The competition is always intense and sometimes cutthroat. And the physical attributes required seem almost inhuman. Simply being attractive is not enough; a model must be both tall and thin and possess excellent teeth, skin, and bone structure. Girls and women should be at least five feet, nine inches tall and around 120 pounds; men should be six feet, two inches tall. Men also need to be jacket size 40 regular or long, waist size 31 to 32, sleeve length 33 to 35, and neck size 15 to 16. Very few human beings on the planet, male or female, have the genetic physical composition required to succeed as a high-fashion model.

While there are more opportunities today—especially for women—in plus-sized, petite, and body-part (such as hand or foot) modeling—the physical requirements for such models are highly specific. And because there are generally fewer modeling opportunities available in these areas than there are in traditional modeling, the competition is fierce.

But for someone with the right look, measurements, and attitude, modeling can be a fantastic career. A successful modeling career can be incredibly lucrative and afford opportunities for world travel; exposure to many interesting people; and sometimes doorways to fame, notoriety, and other exciting careers. Some actresses, like Cameron Diaz and Sharon Stone, as well as actor Nick Nolte, have managed to make a transition from modeling quite successfully. All of these people were probably helped to some degree by the exposure to show business they gained through modeling.

There are no educational requirements for this career, although there are modeling schools and courses that can be helpful, if they are legitimate. Be sure to look into the school's credentials. If it is licensed by the state department of education or is affiliated with a respected agency, it is probably a pretty safe bet. Also try to find out if any of the students have gone on to be successful models. A good modeling school should include courses in wardrobe, hair and makeup, posing, runway walking, acting, and the fashion industry in general.

As with fashion design, it is necessary for a young model to have a good portfolio to show to anyone who will look at it. If you are lucky enough to know a professional photographer or even someone who takes photographs as a hobby and has a good camera, ask if he or she will take some pictures of you. If not, have a friend take a few snapshots.

Most legitimate modeling agents say that they do not necessarily need or even want to see professional photographs, especially if they seem posed and artificial, so it is not worthwhile to spend a huge chunk of money on a photographer or portrait studio. Just pick out two of the best pictures of yourself that you can find, including one head shot and one body shot. A head shot shows only your face and neck, and a body shot shows your entire body, including your legs. Make sure you have enough copies of these pictures to hand out, since you will be shopping them around to modeling agencies. They will often ask you to leave the photos with them, and you will not always get them back.

You can look for agency addresses and phone numbers in your local yellow pages or get started with the ones listed at the back of this book. Contact them first by telephone and ask if they have "open calls," which are a scheduled time when you can bring in your pictures to show to an agent. When you go to an open call, be sure to look your best and bring your photographs to show or drop off. You will get a response either that day or several days later. If you do not live close enough to the agency to go in person, the photos can be sent by mail. Do not take it personally if you are turned down, since you may not be the type that particular agency is looking for.

Be sure to use common sense to protect yourself as you conduct your search. Someone who approaches you out of nowhere claiming to be a modeling agent could be a dangerous person. Many advertisements in magazines and newspapers seeking models are scams. Some people who want to take financial and/or sexual advantage of aspiring models place ads in magazines and newspapers; other people are seeking models who will pose for pornographic pictures. Do not go to any place that does not seem to be a legitimate fashion modeling agency, and never go to the residence of an individual. Professional modeling agents do not operate in this way.

One excellent way to find opportunities and gain exposure in modeling is through conventions. You can find out about these by asking the modeling agencies that you contact and by scanning your local newspaper. A convention usually involves a modeling competition of some sort, and winning can sometimes result in being signed to an agency. Even if you do not win the competition, modeling conventions can bring you into contact with important people in the industry and offer the opportunity to learn from experts how the industry works. Usually these events are intended for young women and men with at least a small amount of modeling experience or training, not for those who are just beginning to take an interest. But if you know that you want to model and feel ready to compete against other young hopefuls in runway shows, photo shoots, and even screen tests, a convention can be excellent experience. It may confirm your confidence as a model, or it may make you realize that this is not the career for you. But it could help to launch your career, especially if you are a winner!

Of course, as with most aspects of modeling, not all conventions are legitimate or even helpful. Try to investigate the event as much as possible, especially before plunking down a fee. After being involved in the fashion industry for a while, investigating everything thoroughly will become second nature as it can be a world full of empty promises. But in the beginning, it is always important not to be too trusting.

What It's Like: An Interview with a Male Model

Kyle is an aspiring photographer in New York City who modeled for four years. His story is a good example of both the exciting benefits and difficult pitfalls of a career in modeling. It also illustrates the importance of networking and preparation.

Kyle began modeling when he was studying visual communications at the Art Institute of Pittsburgh in 1986. He had friends who were photographers, and they agreed to take some test shots of Kyle just to see how they would turn out. When the results turned out to be stunning, Kyle realized that he had the potential to model professionally.

On a suggestion from a friend, Kyle decided to take the photographs to a department store called Kauffman's to show them to the store's art director. The director was skeptical at first since Kyle does not resemble the average, rugged male model in person. But he has a striking, photogenic face with an excellent complexion and nearly perfect bone structure. He also has a tall, lean frame with the perfect measurements to make designer clothes look their best.

"We take only professional models," was the agent's cold response when Kyle first approached him. However, his tone changed when he saw the fantastic shots. He advised Kyle to try his luck in New York and Europe.

So Kyle soon followed up on a modeling agency's newspaper ad that boldly asked, "Want to be a model?" He brought his pictures to the agency, where he met an agent named Linda Ferrari. Linda remains Kyle's friend to this day. The agency told him about a convention that would be taking place at a hotel in Erie, Pennsylvania. The convention included a contest, where Kyle competed in categories like runway walking and photo posing. The contestants also had to write and act out their own commercials. Kyle won first place in the contest and received a prize of $500. An agent at the convention named Ward, who was also a model, told Kyle that he had the right look for an agency in New York City called Click.

So Kyle packed up and left for the big city with only $500 in his pocket. Fortunately, Click quickly agreed to take him on. The agency soon sent him jetting off to Europe, where he modeled in fabulous Paris runway shows for top-name designers, including Jean Paul Gaultier, Comme de Garcons, and Paul Smith. From there he traveled to Milan, Italy, where he worked in print campaigns and commercials. For Kyle it was a dream come true. He was doing things that he had always wanted to do and getting paid to travel to exotic locations and meet exciting and interesting people.

In Milan, Kyle spent much of his time with Courtney, a young female model he had met at the convention. Courtney had been sexually harassed by an agent in Paris and was extremely shaken by the experience. Years later Courtney appeared on the television show *60 Minutes*, where she told her story and exposed the agent.

Kyle's problems began suddenly and without warning. First a very lucrative commercial that his agency had set up for him fell through. The agency never even called to let him know about the cancellation. When he called the agency and asked about it, they coldly replied that it had been an option but was not anymore. Kyle was frustrated and appalled by their behavior.

Soon Kyle's money ran out. He was waiting for payments from runway shows he had worked on in Paris, but the checks did not arrive soon enough. He could not leave Milan because he had come there using a courier ticket, a type of plane ticket that specifies a return date. Kyle's return date was in July, which was four months away. He felt trapped and afraid, and the Italian city seemed cold and ruthless. Many people whom he thought of as friends turned him away. Finally he found someone to loan him a small amount of cash, but once that was gone, he had to sleep on a park bench for several nights.

Kyle returned to his hometown depressed and discouraged. He was not happy there, so he soon flew back to New York, where he worked as a waiter. He also modeled there for about two years, doing print work for magazines such as *YM* and *Details* as well as several commercials.

But Kyle soon became frustrated again with modeling. His portfolio was stolen, and he had a difficult time getting copies of the photographs from the photographers who had taken them. Then his agency closed. He had been slated to return to Milan, a trip the agency had promised to pay for, but that fell through. He was taken in by a new agency that found him work with a popular fashion magazine called *L.A. Style*, but soon that agency also closed. It was then that Kyle decided that it was time to consider other career possibilities.

What did you like most about modeling?

The glamour! It was fun when I was working. I kept thinking, "I can't believe I've done what I set out to do." I was making money, but it didn't feel like I was really doing anything with my time. I roamed around Paris and Milan, seeing the city and making money. I had always wanted to see Europe. And runway shows were fantastic. It was exciting being showered with flashes from the paparazzi. I met a lot of celebrities and designers whom I admired. I did everything I had set out to do, and even more.

What did you like least about it?

I did not like all of the vain and crass people in the industry and the coldness and indifference. The business is always running hot and cold about different looks. One minute you're in; the next minute you're out. And I encountered a lot of dishonesty.

What did you gain from modeling that still helps you to this day?

It did a lot for my self-confidence. I had a dream, and I made it happen. I did have some bad experiences, but I now have those to draw on. I have a certain amount of faith in my dreams as a result. I did my part, and I know that if I did it again, I could get what I want. Also, I learned that looks are not everything.

Do you have any words of advice for young people interested in getting into modeling?

Forget it! Go to school. But if it really is something you want to do, try to figure out why you want it. If it is only to be famous and it is not something you really believe in, you'll probably have trouble with it. If you decide it is for you, then it is best to plan ahead and have a lot of money set aside. Since you may not work in the beginning, you need to have a cushion to fall back on. And you have to believe in it and follow through. Nobody will do it for you, and usually the agents just want their 20 percent. If they think they can make a lot of money through you, then challenge them on that. And if they are willing to front you enough money and you are willing to work hard without becoming lazy or getting a big head, you will go somewhere. It is possible. It happens all the time, and from my point of view, it is not unusual.

What about modeling was different from what you expected before you started?

It was an odd combination of amazement and disappointment. I had not really expected such an enthusiastic response from people. Being in that environment was better than I had expected, in that I felt as though I had a right to be there. I worked hard and saved money, working as a waiter when I would rather have been doing something else. Being in the modeling world was the payoff.

If you could do it again, what would you do differently?

I would be more financially prepared. I would also work on "Model Kyle," meaning I would work harder on expressing myself with style. That is what gets you someplace. I would be more conscious of what I wore, and I would save some money to buy a good designer suit. I would have something to back me up while I was modeling. Since I have learned a lot about photography since that time, maybe I would photograph other models in my spare time. I would not want to depend upon modeling for my entire income because that takes a lot of the pleasure out of it.

Young modeling hopefuls in the United States without much experience sometimes think, "Oh, I'll just take off for Europe and make huge amounts of money modeling there, because it's easy overseas. Then I'll come back to America and get tons of offers because of all my international experience." Some successful models have no doubt taken this approach, but it can be dangerous not to have a standby plan to fall back on. And modeling in Europe is definitely not an easy thing to do.

It can be difficult to leave your home and everything familiar to you behind to adapt to a totally new environment, especially one where you do not speak the language. Running out of money can be devastating, and no young model should leave the country without at least $2,000 in the bank. There can be problems with airlines and luggage—not to mention the common problem of rejection, which is compounded when you have no friends or family around. Health insurance is another consideration—illness or accidents can happen anywhere. To be hospitalized in a foreign country with no way to pay for it can be terrifying.

On the plus side, modeling in Europe with enough money, a workable plan, a trustworthy agent, and a sense of responsibility can be an exciting way to see the world. You can gain exposure to other cultures and ways of thinking that are new to you. And there are more opportunities for new models in Europe than in the United States because there are more fashion houses and magazines there. The experience young models gain in Europe is invaluable to their careers and is sometimes exactly what they need to become noticed in the United States. There is no guarantee that it will work that way, of course, but for the right person, it can.

Makeup Artistry

The other girls at Janet's high school always admired her makeup. She looked flawless yet completely natural. Whereas the other girls struggled with lines that would not blend, eye shadow that clashed with their lipstick, foundation that was always too light or too heavy, and mascara that gobbed uncontrollably, Janet seemed to apply her makeup effortlessly. When the girls asked Janet what her secret was, she just laughed and said that she enjoyed doing makeup. She actually worked at it, spending hours practicing on herself and her friends. It never occurred to Janet that this skill might be valuable to her in the future.

Some people have a knack for applying cosmetics, and there is a tremendous need for these people in the fashion industry. Models do not look perfect and glossy when they show up for a shoot. Makeup has a lot to do with a model's look and can help to set the entire mood for a set of photographs or runway show. Some clothing designers want a particular collection of apparel to be shown with shiny cosmetics, or a photographer may feel that makeup should be as light and natural as possible for a certain background. Makeup artists must satisfy these demands to make sure that the model looks spectacular when the flashbulbs go off.

Many successful makeup artists say that the best way to learn how to apply makeup is through trial and error. Experiment on your own face, and on friends, relatives, and anyone else who will let you. Kevyn Aucoin, one of today's top makeup artists, was fascinated by cosmetics at a very early age. When he was just eleven, he would apply lipstick to his five-year-old sister, Carla. He was amazed at how different it made her look.

Makeup jobs are available in both commercial and theatrical areas. Commercial work includes doing makeup for cosmetic companies and salons, and for anything else that involves facing the public. Theatrical work involves makeup for staged productions as well as television and film. It also requires more training than commercial work, as the makeup artist needs to learn about cinematography, sculpturing, plastics, and many special procedures, such as call sheets and script breakdown.

Many beauty schools offer courses in makeup, but a formal education is not always required to land a job in commercial makeup. The curricula for these schools are constantly subject to change because the cosmetics industry changes so frequently. Courses generally focus on both artistry and products and how cosmetics are applied in demonstrations, sales, photography, and theatrical productions.

Anyone going into this career should obtain a cosmetology license, although it is not always required. In some states it is illegal to do makeup for pay without one, and some companies require that anyone they hire have a license, regardless of state laws. This license can be obtained from your state's department of commerce. A test and fee are usually required for licensing, as well as a high school or general equivalency diploma (GED). For commercial work, all that is required is a facialist license, which is not very expensive or difficult to get. It is more difficult to get a license to do theatrical work than for commercial work. To work on a large theatrical production, a makeup artist may also be required to be a member of a union.

There are many excellent ways for a young, aspiring makeup artist to gain experience. One of the best ways is to find photographers and models that are young, inexperienced, and building up their own portfolios. This makes more sense than trying to jump right in with the professionals for your first shoots. Young photographers and models can be contacted through art schools, fashion schools, universities, and community bulletin boards. Usually they will be excited to work with you, and you may get some excellent photographs to start a portfolio of your own.

Of course, as with many fashion professions, the apprenticeship route is always a possibility. Apprenticeships with film and television studios are very difficult to get. A slightly easier route is to find an experienced makeup artist to assist. You will probably have to work for free at first, but you can learn the art of makeup and the workings of the career firsthand.

Working at a cosmetics counter in a department store or boutique can also provide valuable experience. Many stores will train you in makeup application, but even if they do not, it is a great way to work with cosmetics, apply them to many different faces, and possibly get discounts on makeup.

A discount can be important when it comes to stocking your own makeup kit. If you are taking makeup courses, you may be required to buy a kit through the school. This can cost between $100 and $200. As you begin to work and gain more experience, you will figure out which cosmetics and brands work best for you. As a professional, you may at any given time have over $1,000 worth of makeup with you on the job! Some professionals spend from $300 to $500 a month on cosmetics, which comes from their own pockets if they work as freelancers.

Fashion Retailing

Jennifer could sell anything to anybody. By the time she was seventeen, she had worked part-time at several retail jobs. Of all the salespeople, Jennifer always earned the highest commissions. As she got older, she decided that her future was probably in some kind of sales, but she was not sure what she wanted to sell. She was interested in fashion, and she considered selling clothing. But she also wondered if there were other possibilities. How else could she be involved in fashion and sales?

Textile Sales

Textile sales, also referred to as fabric sales, is a fast-paced and challenging career option. A textile salesperson may sell fibers for making yarn, yarn for making fabric, or actual finished fabrics for making clothing and furniture. This means that the salesperson deals with many kinds of people, from yarn and fabric manufacturers to fashion designers and apparel manufacturers.

Textile salespeople must possess tremendous knowledge of the products being sold and know all there is to know about the companies they represent. They must also be effective communicators to convey all their knowledge about their products to the customers. Finally, they must be friendly and persuasive. Many salespeople work on commission, which means that they make a percentage of the profit for their sales, so a "sales personality" is a must to survive.

What is a sales personality? Assertiveness is one trait, but the line between assertive and obnoxious must not be crossed. An ability to deal with pressure and rejection is essential. And you should enjoy working with people since the position is really about communicating information and forming relationships. An impatient or unsociable person would probably go completely bonkers doing this kind of work.

If you decide to pursue this career, you will probably start out as a trainee with a fiber company, yarn company, or textile firm. Training programs vary from company to company, but they usually involve assisting and watching a more experienced salesperson at work for a period of time. This gives the trainee a chance to learn the company's product line as well as sales techniques and to gain an understanding of the customers' needs. There may be clerical duties such as light accounting, typing, and order entry.

The position of textile salesperson may also involve some door-to-door type selling. Sometimes the salesperson may go to potential or established customers with samples to show. This provides a constant change of surroundings, which can be perfect for people who do not like to work in the same room all day long. Travel out of the city or even the state may also be required, which is an attractive idea for some.

Clothing Sales

Alex loved his summer job at the Gap. He loved working with clothing, and he knew that he wanted to be a part of the fashion world after he graduated from high school. He was not sure exactly what he wanted to do, and he was considering several possibilities. Fashion design sounded interesting, but he also loved taking photographs. Marketing and promotion seemed like it might be fun, too.

It all seemed very confusing, and Alex realized that it might take him a little while to make up his mind. Fortunately, his boss at the Gap really liked him and offered him a management job after he graduated. Alex decided to take the job since it would be good experience while he was thinking about his next step. He had already learned so much from working in retail. He wondered how high he could climb on the career ladder starting as a salesperson.

Working as a salesperson in a department store or boutique is an excellent start for anyone interested in working in fashion. Most of us are already familiar with what salespeople do. Primarily they assist customers in finding the merchandise they want and gently persuade them to buy the product. They usually have additional responsibilities to occupy their time when not selling, such as folding or stocking.

In the preceding section on textile sales, you learned what it means to have a sales personality. Someone who works as a salesperson in a department store must develop these same traits. A salesperson must have the intelligence to know and fully understand the store's product, the communication skills to convey the information to the customers, and the personality and charm to persuade customers to buy without being irritating or intimidating. This is a difficult balance to strike, and not everybody can do it.

But for those with the skills, personality, and stamina, retail sales can be a rewarding job that opens doors to many career paths. The hours may be difficult, especially for someone just getting started, and often involve working late nights and weekends. Of course, working at the same store for a length of time affords a salesperson a bit of seniority, which sometimes leads to more desirable work hours, but not always. Many people do not mind working nights and weekends because it keeps them out of the routine of the nine-to-five world.

Many entry-level sales positions are part-time only, which can be ideal for someone in high school or college if the store management team is flexible. Almost all salespeople work on commission. Their base salary is low, generally an hourly rate ranging from $5 to $10, plus a percentage of what they sell. The hourly rate may be higher depending on the price level of the department store. However, retail jobs at designer stores or prestigious department stores like Saks Fifth Avenue are much more difficult to come by than jobs at lower-level stores. The more prestigious and expensive stores usually require previous retail experience from their salespeople.

Starting at the bottom can be frustrating, but it is necessary for people who want to get a foot in the door of the fashion world, no matter how creative and talented they are. The bottom is where you learn the skills necessary to take you to the top. As long as you keep an open mind and really make an effort to learn all you can in this position, it will not take long to move up. And it can be a fun and fascinating source of income for students.

The Long, Hard Road to Store Management

When Alex graduated he took the management job at the Gap, as he had planned. The position was assistant manager. He spent the first few days following the store manager around and paying attention to what she was doing. She told him that as soon as he was trained, Alex would be promoted to department manager. He liked several things about management, such as being responsible for a team of employees and organizing sales and promotions. He still was not sure if this was the exact fashion career he wanted, but he thought the skills he was learning would be extremely useful no matter what he ultimately decided to do. And maybe store management would be where he wanted to stay.

Many successful people in the fashion industry, from buyers to designers, began their careers as store managers. This position is considered an excellent springboard to many exciting fashion jobs and can also be the perfect career in itself for the right person. It can be an extremely challenging and sometimes exhausting position. Running a department store is a major responsibility no matter how large or small the store is. Your actions as store manager can have a tremendous effect on a large company's rate of success.

The first step on the ladder to store manager is assistant department manager, which is basically the title you assume while training to be a department manager. This position usually consists of nothing more than watching and assisting the department manager as he or she performs various tasks. Once promoted to department manager, you become responsible for supervising your staff, including salespeople and stock handlers. You need to keep the staff informed of anything special that might be happening in the store, such as sales and promotions. The department manager sometimes hires and trains new employees. All of these things require a worker with excellent people skills as well as absolute knowledge of all aspects of the store's operations.

The department manager usually works closely with the buyers to make sure the merchandise bought for the store is presented in a way that attracts and appeals to customers. Sometimes the department manager performs tasks that are similar to those of the buyer's. We will discuss the buyer's responsibilities in a later section.

Department managers often spend their days buried in paperwork, analyzing sales and inventory figures. They also work with customers every day, so again, patience and solid people skills are required. The department manager must also keep a sharp eye on the salespeople to make sure their interactions with customers run smoothly. Occasionally he or she may need to step in to solve a problem that has become too complicated for the salesperson to solve or to soothe an irate customer.

Department managers can expect a starting salary ranging anywhere from $18,000 to $25,000 yearly. In addition to that salary, most department managers have opportunities to earn bonuses based on success in sales, inventory, or personnel.

The department manager reports to the group manager. Salaries for group managers range from $25,000 to $40,000, and the duties are not unlike those of department managers. The only real difference is increased responsibility and more management duties.

From group manager the next step can be either operations manager or personnel manager. The operations manager is responsible for much of the store's maintenance and appearance as well as security. This position also includes customer service; receiving merchandise and supplies; handling credit, refund, and exchange transactions; and gift wrapping.

The personnel manager works closely with all employees. Responsibilities in this position include interviewing potential candidates for various positions, placing employees in the proper departments and evaluating their performance, training employees, and scheduling. The personnel manager may also discipline employees when necessary and deal with benefits programs such as insurance and time off.

The next step up from personnel or operations manager is, finally, store manager. Of course, in smaller stores, the ladder to store manager may be much shorter because there are fewer employees making up the rungs. For example, a department manager may be promoted directly to store manager and be expected to assume the roles of both personnel and operations manager. As with most fashion retailing careers, the specifics largely depend upon the structure of each store.

Because he or she is at the top of the ladder, the store manager is responsible for pretty much everything and everyone in the store. He or she must manage the salespeople, department managers, buyers, group managers, operations managers, and personnel managers. He or she must also know what each of these jobs entails and what is going on in the store at all times. The store manager must understand not only how to put out any fires that might start but also how to prevent them from happening. The buck stops with the store manager.

For taking on this huge responsibility, store managers are well compensated. Average salaries for this position begin at $50,000 yearly and can skyrocket into the six-figure range with experience.

Buying

Alex left the Gap after spending three years as store manager. He moved to Los Angeles, a city in which he had always wanted to live, and began working as a manager at Macy's. He loved the atmosphere and enjoyed working with his staff and customers. He made a good salary and was happy in the position, but after about a year, he started to think about new challenges.

Alex heard that a buyer position was opening up, and he wondered if buying might be for him. He did not know much about it except that the buyer selects the clothes for the store to display and sell.

People often referred to buying as a "glamour profession" because it involved a lot of travel, often to exotic locations. He had also heard that being a buyer was an open doorway into the best fashion parties. It sounded exciting, but he wondered what the reality was.

Buying is another fashion career that many people think of as being exciting and glamorous. And like most fashion careers, it can be exciting, glamorous, and more. The "more" part is what throws most people off. Buying is extremely demanding, sometimes even grueling, and requires excellent business and accounting skills. Buyers work with enormous budgets, negotiate with some tough vendors, and make important decisions that affect many people. It is an extremely taxing and high-pressure career.

On the plus side, buying can be exciting for someone with the right personality and the necessary financial skills. Buyers often travel, and they sometimes attend fashion shows of big-name designers. Some buyers do become important figures in the thrilling, fabulous world of haute couture. With hard work, determination, and the right connections, there is no limit to where you can go and what you can achieve on this career path.

So what does a buyer do? Buyers have many responsibilities, and their duties may vary somewhat depending on where they work. Their primary responsibility is deciding which items to purchase for their store and which vendors to purchase from. Buyers may work from the store itself or from the store's corporate office.

A buyer usually does not view the merchandise at a fashion show. It is more common to visit a showroom, where a vendor holds up the garments and gives the buyer information such as prices, colors, and availability. Buyers must decide quickly whether they want the item, and if so, how many. This requires an ability to think on your feet, to process information, and to make good decisions in just a few seconds.

You may wonder what qualities a buyer looks for in a garment or accessory. This is where technical knowledge of clothing construction comes into play, another trait buyers must possess to succeed. Buyers inspect the clothing to make sure it is well constructed. They must also be experts on their customers' needs, since they must know what will and will not sell. They cannot base their decisions on their own opinions of the clothing. Buyers need to understand what is happening in the overall fashion market and how it pertains to their specific customer base.

For example, what does it mean to upper-class women in their forties and fifties that hip-hop fashion is hot in this month's *Vogue* and on the runways? A lack of understanding of these complex relationships as well as the workings of the industry could result in poor judgment and some disastrous decisions! Buyers must also have the foresight to know in advance what their customers will want in the future, sometimes as far as six months ahead.

But selecting clothing is really only about 10 percent of what a buyer does. Most of a buyer's time is spent crunching numbers. If you are thinking about exploring this career, you should be ready for some serious financial analysis and accounting. Most people who stick with this position were not looking for something creative, and anyone going into it should understand that it is mostly business.

The buyer is responsible for predicting sales and profits and for estimating how much inventory the company will need. He or she does this by analyzing various figures and accounting reports. He or she must be able to come up with an accurate figure that shows how much can and should be spent to achieve the predicted profits. All of this requires strong analytical and mathematical skills and a degree and experience in the field of accounting.

After establishing a budget, the buyer must also track sales and inventory using computer-generated reports. It is the buyer that must determine how well he or she is doing and what could be done differently to bring about greater profits. Sometimes it is a matter of ordering different items, different quantities, or a combination of the two. Buyers must be able to use their own fashion expertise and common sense to interpret what the accounting reports are telling them about their choices.

As a buyer, you will work with different kinds of people. You will be involved with the display and promotion of the merchandise you buy, which will put you into contact with salespeople, advertising departments, and visual merchandisers. You may also be responsible for contributing to the development of new products for your company. This is more common in large, established department stores that have the budget and reputation to develop their own lines of clothing.

The most common route to a job as a buyer is to start out working as a salesperson in a department store, then work up to store manager. From there you have a good shot at an assistant buyer position, which can give you an idea of what the buyer position is really like. As an assistant buyer, you would be expected to do a lot of paperwork and analysis. If you stay in this position for a while, more responsibilities will be allocated to you as well as more interesting work. You may even be able to travel with the buyer. As an assistant, it is important to soak up as much information as possible. It can take anywhere from six months to three years to advance to the position of buyer.

As a buyer, you are not entirely limited to department stores for employment. There are also companies called resident buying offices. These offices basically act as links between department store buyers and the marketplace. Many department stores pay resident buying offices to help their buyers find and promote merchandise and sometimes to perform other related services. Salaries paid by resident buying offices are generally lower than wages paid by department stores.

Assistant buyers usually begin making between $18,000 and $30,000 yearly. Those promoted to buyer may earn from $25,000 to $80,000. The next step after buyer is DMM, or divisional merchandise manager, who manages a team of buyers. Salaries for this position range from $35,000 to $90,000. The DMM may then move up to GMM, or general merchandise manager. The GMM manages the entire merchandising division. Some buyers complain that the DMM and GMM get most of the interesting work, while the buyer is stuck simply gathering information. Whether or not this is the case depends largely on the way each individual store is set up.

Sales Representative

Since he had accumulated so much experi-
ence in retail and had enjoyed it so much,
Alex decided he would rather set his sights on
a sales representative position. He enjoyed
working with people and liked the challenge
of trying to persuade them to buy something
from him. He also liked the idea of working
on commission because he knew the money
would motivate him to do his best. It seemed
like a job that suited his personality in many
ways and would constantly challenge him.

Sales representatives in fashion complement the buyers, because it is their job to sell merchandise to stores. Sales reps contact buyers and try to persuade them to look at the clothing made by the designer or firm they work for. They may do this from showrooms or their own homes, but the reps who work from home generally travel a great deal to bring samples directly to buyers.

Since it is a sales job, those going into this field should be assertive but not overly aggressive. Enthusiasm, friendliness, interpersonal communication skills, and persuasiveness are important. A pleasant telephone manner and conversational ability should come naturally to a sales representative. A proactive attitude is also a must—this means you have to be able to take initiative and make things happen rather than waiting to be instructed by your employer to make your next move. You need to be able to go out and grab a sale and not rely on a customer coming to you.

Networking is also important, and relationships with clients need to be built and maintained both on and off company hours. Being a fashion sales representative is not a nine-to-five job, since your schedule revolves largely around those of the buyers. Reps should be in tune with the ever-changing cycles of fashion and learn all there is to know about the products their company is selling. They must also keep a close eye on the competition since it is up to the representatives to make their products look better, newer, and more exciting than all the others. Marketing skills can be extremely advantageous in this job.

Although sales rep is a position on the business end of the fashion career spectrum, personal style and outward appearance are extremely important. A sales representative must have a wardrobe that shows not only knowledge of what's going on in fashion but an ability to apply it realistically to his or her own daily life. If a sales rep cannot even put together an outfit to wear to a meeting, a buyer is unlikely to trust him or her to sell clothing for an entire company.

As a sales representative, you would probably work either partly or entirely on commission. Working on commission means that how much you earn depends on how much you sell. Reps generally earn a commission of 6 to 10 percent of their sales, but some experienced reps earn as much as 15 percent. This figure can vary depending on whether you work in a showroom or on the road. Showroom reps generally earn lower commission along with a weekly salary. Road reps earn a higher commission without the salary.

When an up cycle in your sales turns downward, things can get pretty depressing and even downright scary. Fashion is an up-and-down business, which means that some down times are inevitable. A rep needs to have the foresight to deal with such times financially and the confidence and determination to keep working at it until sales pick up again. A knack for scheduling and map reading may also be necessary, especially for road reps. And as with most jobs, computer skills have become increasingly important.

Both men and women have equal chances to be hired as reps, and there is no formal education required for this career. However, a degree from a marketing or fashion school can give you an edge over the competition, particularly when it comes to advancement into management. There are no limits to how high you can advance from the position of sales rep—from supervisor or assistant sales manager to regional manager, then anywhere up to president of the firm.

There is some tough competition when vying for these positions, but generally a lot of openings exist for sales reps because turnover is high. A good way to find a position is by starting out at any available entry-level position at a manufacturing firm, a design firm, or with an individual designer. Working as a receptionist or sales rep's assistant can give you a good idea of how the sales department works if you pay close attention. You may be lucky enough to get into a good training program on the job, and sometimes a firm is willing to pay employees' fashion school tuition.

The specific duties of sales reps go beyond simply showing clothes to buyers. They must prepare merchandise packages, which include sketches, swatches of fabric, press clips, and photos as well as clothing samples. Reps also write up orders, make sure they are shipped, and sometimes send packages to buyers. Often reps will help organize special promotional events for the store, like fashion shows and sales.

Perks of the job can include the use of a company car, reimbursement for travel, and often a budget for meals and entertainment when traveling. Of course, there generally are also discounts on merchandise.

Window Display Design

Gillian was an art student looking for part-time work in Chicago. She loved fashion and had many friends who were models and photographers. One of them suggested that she look for work in window display design. She noticed an ad in the newspaper for an assistant to the window designer at Bloomingdale's. Starting pay was only $5 an hour with room for advancement. Gillian wanted more money, but she decided to take the position anyway in the hope that she would eventually get a raise if she did well.

After a few days, Gillian knew that she had made the right decision. Instead of sweeping floors or flipping burgers to get through school, she could paint, sew, and brainstorm for ideas and concepts. Her creativity was engaged, and she found the work stimulating. She also hit it off with the head designer, who gave her many responsibilities and promised to give her a raise within a month. He even let her exhibit her own paintings in the displays. Gillian could not imagine a better part-time job, and she thought she might even try it out full-time after she graduated.

Have you ever glanced at a department store window and wondered who created the fantastic artwork behind the mannequins or the clever concept that pulled the outfits together and drew your attention to the clothes being displayed? This is the work of an artistic, fashion-conscious individual called a window display designer. Designing window displays can be an excellent starting point for someone with aspirations on the top of the fashion ladder, or it can be a great career all on its own. It is a job that allows for creative expression, constant exposure to large audiences, and tremendous potential for high salary growth and advancement. It also puts artistic and creative impulses to work directly in a retail environment.

The entry-level position for this career is called trimmer or assistant to the designer. Trimmers spend most of their time painting backdrops or covering them with fabric, dressing mannequins, finding and setting up props for the display, and doing anything else the designer requests. Unfortunately the starting salary for this position is extremely low, sometimes as low as minimum wage. But a trimmer who has great ideas and shares them frequently will usually be promoted quickly. A trimmer should also spend some time putting together a portfolio, a book that includes photographs of windows that he or she has worked on.

If an assistant is promoted to designer, a raise is generally part of the promotion. Designers develop concepts for the windows, sketch their ideas and sometimes create blueprints, and supervise other staff, including carpenters, painters, and trimmers. Brainstorming for ideas is something a designer must do at all times, since potential ideas are everywhere. Movies, plays, art museums, television, and magazines are all excellent sources of inspiration for displays, so even a certain amount of a designer's leisure time is spent working. Most creative people are accustomed to working this way.

Some people attend art or fashion school to prepare for a career as a window display designer, which is helpful but not necessary. A good way to get exposure in window display without a formal education is to get a job as a department store salesperson first, then offer to help with the window displays.

Designers have the option of working on staff at one department store or freelancing with as many stores as possible. Freelancers usually get jobs through word of mouth, so establishing a reputation is important for those taking this route. Whereas staff designers usually have enough props available in the store to use in their displays, freelance designers must find their own props and backdrops at thrift stores and flea markets. Sometimes a designer will make a deal with another store to borrow a prop, such as a piece of furniture, in exchange for a mention of the supplier's name somewhere in the display. This provides free materials for the designer to work with as well as free advertising for the supplier.

Anyone who is considering becoming a window display designer should have some artistic ability as well as knowledge of art concepts such as depth, perspective, composition, and color. Graphic design is also important because many window displays require the use of symbols, lines, and lettering. And of course, a window designer should enjoy keeping up-to-date on the latest fashion trends so their displays can stay one step ahead of the competition.

A window display designer does not necessarily need to be a skilled carpenter, but he or she should definitely be familiar with a toolbox. Basic painting skills are also necessary, mainly for use with backdrops and props. Because the importance of lighting in presenting merchandise attractively cannot be overestimated, a window display designer needs to be able to use light to its best advantage. It is extremely helpful if the designer can also do the wiring, but this is not absolutely necessary. Finally, a designer must have the vision to imagine how the window should look and the drive to see it through to completion.

Although a job in window display is not necessarily easy to get, competition for this career is not especially fierce. Working hours for freelancers are difficult to gauge and can include some night and weekend work. Employment by a department store does not guarantee a nine-to-five schedule, but the hours are generally more regular. Staff designers with department stores also sometimes receive benefits like health insurance, vacation days, and discounts on merchandise. The busiest time of the year is the holiday season, between October and January.

Fashion
Journalism

5

Writing had always come easily for Jeffrey. He took many English and creative writing courses in school and was on the staff of his school's newspaper and yearbook. He found that he much preferred writing the fun, entertainment-oriented newspaper pieces to hard news stories. He thought he might be interested in working as a journalist for a living, but news did not thrill him in the slightest. He had a difficult time keeping up with current events—how could he possibly be a journalist? If only he could write about something that interested him, like fashion.

For those who want to combine a talent for writing with a serious fashion fascination, there are many opportunities in the fashion world for exciting careers. One of the primary ways fashion is promoted in the media is through magazines. This does not only include strictly fashion-oriented magazines such as *Vogue, Harper's*

Bazaar, and *Elle*. Fashion-related articles and features can be found in magazines such as *Spin* and *Rolling Stone*, and even in *Time* and *Newsweek*, as well as in the daily newspapers in larger cities. Fashion is an important part of our culture, and gifted writers and editors are always needed to convey and shape ideas about it.

One opportunity for a writer interested in fashion is the position of fashion journalist. Fashion journalists report on all aspects of the fashion industry, which include much more than just clothing. There is a vast array of potentially interesting stories to be revealed about accessories, fragrances, cosmetics, trends, and the fascinating and eccentric personalities that make up the fashion world.

Someone aspiring to the position of fashion journalist should have excellent writing and editing skills as well as immense knowledge of the fashion industry and how it works. Fashion journalists need to be familiar with all of the trends and happenings before anyone else picks up on them, as they are the ones keeping the rest of us posted. It is also necessary to have computer experience and skills; many journalists give their ideas shape using word processing and desktop publishing programs.

An ability to work under pressure is essential, as all magazine publishers give their writers firm deadlines. When a writer is given a date for a story to be finished, there is no excuse accepted for turning it in late. The entire publication depends on the writer to produce a fresh, insightful, and grammatically and factually correct story and to do it quickly and efficiently.

If this seems more challenging and exciting than intimidating to you, it might be a good direction to consider. Sometimes, there can be glamorous moments in this career, including travel to exotic locations, encounters and interviews with celebrities, and high-profile events and parties. Of course, the glamour always goes hand-in-hand with extremely hard work.

Prepare for this career by taking as many English and journalism classes as possible. Other good courses include creative writing, literature, and home economics classes such as textiles and apparel. Most schools have a newspaper and yearbook staff that you can join to gain valuable experience in writing, reporting, and working within deadlines. Working as a salesperson or clerk in a clothing store is also a good idea because it will keep you posted on new styles that are popular and what the public is looking for.

Study fashion magazines very closely. Read all of the articles and pay close attention to what they are about and how they are put together. Analyze the structure of the stories, what style of writing is being used, and what buzzwords keep popping up again and again. Fashion journalists should be aware of these things. Subscribe to your favorite magazines and save the articles that you think are exceptionally well written and interesting.

There are certain educational requirements for the career of fashion journalism. At least four years of college with a major in English, journalism, or communications is necessary for a chance at breaking into this highly competitive field. Experience in retail sales is also helpful, as well as classes in computer literacy, word processing, and desktop publishing.

There are internships available to college students at many newspapers and magazines. An internship can be beneficial in many ways. Aside from providing valuable practical experience, an internship can lead to exceptional networking opportunities and job prospects after school. Some companies hire their interns as full-time employees after they graduate.

There are different ways to go about hunting down a job as a fashion journalist. The first option, which requires a considerable amount of nerve, is to search for fashion editors at trade shows and other fashion events. Ask for a business card, then give the magazine a call to find out when they have a minute to speak with you. Introduce yourself and ask if you can send them some writing samples. A follow-up call a couple of weeks later is also a good idea.

Another possibility is to start out freelancing. This means that you do not work for a specific publication but rather come up with your own ideas for stories and pitch them to various magazines using query letters that explain and sell your ideas to magazine editors. If someone likes your idea, you may get paid ahead of time to follow through and write the story for the magazine. Or you can simply write a story, skip the query letter, and just send copies of the story out to several publications. These are good ways to create an impressive file of your published clips, which increases your chances of obtaining a full-time staff writer position. Many people build solid, successful careers doing only freelance work.

Many cities have small, local, style-related publications, which can be excellent places for the aspiring fashion journalist to start. Your local newspaper's style section is also a good bet. If your ideas are fresh, your writing sparkles, and you know how to network, you have a good chance of being published in some of the country's top fashion publications someday.

Starting salaries for fashion journalists range from $18,000 to $20,000 yearly and can increase with experience to $30,000 and beyond for writers at the top publications. Also included in your pay may be discounts on fabulous clothes and accessories as well as paid travel to exciting locations. This is a growing profession, especially with the advent of online magazines (magazines that can be accessed only on the Internet), and new possibilities continue to emerge.

Another career path for fashion writers is the position of catalog copywriter. Writing for catalogs is challenging because the small blurbs of information that describe the products have to be extremely concise as well as persuasive. In most cases, hours for copywriters are close to the standard nine-to-five schedule, as opposed to the unpredictable hustle and bustle of journalism. Catalog writers may work on-staff or freelance for stores and mail-order companies.

Copywriters who work mainly in catalogs may be able to move into the field of advertising, writing copy for ad agencies. There are also many opportunities opening up in cyberspace for this type of writing.

If you think you might be interested in a copywriting career, you can begin preparing in basically the same ways that an aspiring fashion journalist would. But in addition to reading and collecting articles from fashion magazines, check out as many catalogs as possible. Study the writing in the columns and under the photographs, and try to understand what the writer is attempting to accomplish in the small space that is allotted. Pay close attention to word choices and the gentle persuasion that is put into the writing, much like the words of a salesperson in a store trying to secure a sale to a customer.

Educational requirements are not as strict for catalog copywriters. As long as you have the skills, most employers will not necessarily expect you to have a degree in writing or English. Of course, writing classes are helpful, as is working for school newspapers and yearbooks. Perhaps you could gain some experience in promotion by designing fliers for a local band or helping to promote school events.

Once you are ready to start looking for a job in the field, gather your writing clips together and send the best ones to advertising agencies and mail-order catalog companies with cover letters and résumés. You may need to start out writing for nonfashion catalogs, but do not be discouraged if you end up describing power tools and lawn ornaments. The more experience you get, the more power you will have in deciding what kinds of products you want to write about, and the closer you can move to the fashion industry. Salaries may start at $17,000 to $20,000 annually and increase to around $30,000 or more with experience.

Fashion Photography

Will finally felt as though he had found his dream job. He traveled all over the world, met interesting and influential people, and could be as creative and artistic as he wanted. And the pay was not too bad either. He had been a photographer for Gloss *magazine for six months and had already photographed three top models. He had just found out that he might be photographing Sharon Stone next month! The hours were a bit unpredictable, but Will enjoyed the spontaneity. This job had not been easy to get, and he had spent several years carrying around his portfolio, showing his photos to anyone who would look. He had also interned for almost no money at a small entertainment weekly, and he had come very close to giving up several times. Now his hard work was paying off, and he truly appreciated his success.*

Photography is one of the most powerful and essential components of fashion. Fashion photographs are recognized as art, and in some cases as great art. A photograph largely determines how a dress or other article of clothing looks. And it is the most common and effective way for fashion images to be disseminated to the masses of people who buy the merchandise. This type of photography can be imaginative, striking, and incredibly influential.

Fashion photography can be a dream come true for a creative person with a good eye and a sense of glamour. Some people have a natural instinct for photographing other people well and for helping them to look their best. Many photographers have become modern celebrities, like Herb Ritts, David LaChapelle, Steven Meisel, and Ellen von Unwerth, to name just a few. These are individuals who are recognized for their unique style and skillful work in fashion photography. Their images grace both magazines and art gallery walls. In fact, many people credit these photographers and others like them for creating art that is accessible to everyone in every setting, from museums to grocery stores.

It is easy to romanticize a career in fashion photography, but the job is definitely not all about glamour and fun. Most photographers love what they are doing for a living, but they have to work extremely hard and deal with a tremendous amount of pressure and rejection. This is a career that only becomes more fast-paced and furious as you become more successful. Competition is razor sharp when you are shooting a high-profile fashion show in Paris or trying to land a photo shoot with a top model for a magazine like *Elle*. If you are someone who thrives on competition, this aspect of the job should be no problem, but if not, you might want to think about doing something else. The hours are also extremely long and unpredictable, so do not expect a nine-to-five schedule.

If you think that you may be interested in a career as a fashion photographer, try to learn as much about taking photographs as you possibly can. Like aspiring fashion writers, you must become an avid collector of magazines. Buy fashion magazines as well as other magazines and newspapers that have fashion sections and layouts. Even photo shoots of celebrities that accompany interviews and feature stories are good to examine. Create scrapbooks of your favorite images. Take note of what qualities in the subjects the photographs seem to capture, and try to imagine how this was done. Look at the angles that are used as well as lighting and surrounding colors, and how both of these elements complement the model and his or her clothing. A fashion photographer must be a master of all of these complex techniques.

You will need to buy a camera to start experimenting on your own. Even if all you can afford is a simple camera to take snapshots, everyone needs to start somewhere. Take the camera everywhere you go and grab any photo opportunities that come up. Try to achieve the same effects you see in magazines by testing out unusual angles.

Eventually you will need to invest in a professional camera with some basic features, as well as a few simple lighting fixtures. It can be fun to invite your friends over to dress up and have their pictures taken. Coordinate miniature photo shoots in your backyard or basement, and experiment with backdrops using sheets and blankets of different colors. Aluminum foil and plastic wrap can create some interesting effects on film as well.

Other ways to get involved with photography are school yearbooks and newspapers. Some schools also have photography clubs, which can be excellent places to discuss photography methods and techniques with others who are also just getting started. Try to get a part-time job in a photo-developing center, even just working at the counter or being a "gofer." If you keep your eyes and ears open, you should be able to pick up a lot of useful information and possibly even meet people who can help you get started in your career.

Eventually you may be able to find an experienced photographer to apprentice with. In exchange for your assistance with simple tasks like deliveries and cleaning, a photographer may be willing to pass on invaluable information to you about taking photographs as well as about getting your foot in the door of the business. This is one of the most effective ways to be educated for this career.

It is also important to earn a college degree in photography, especially if your goal is to work for magazines. There are schools that specialize in photography, although most colleges simply have a photography department and offer it as a major. It is extremely difficult to find a job in photojournalism if you do not have a college degree. With extraordinary talent anything is possible, but it is strongly advised that anyone going into this career receive some formal training.

Photographers must possess strong technical ability so that they can understand and utilize equipment that is often complicated and confusing. They need to be creative and imaginative, perpetually bursting with fantastic ideas. They should also be willing to travel great distances and on short notice.

Fashion photographers need to be able to think on their feet and to convey their ideas on the spot: "Stand like this. OK, go stand on that. Great, now try holding this. That's beautiful; hold it there. Move to the left. Perfect." Working with models requires excellent people skills. The photographer must develop a relationship with the model that is based on trust so that the model feels comfortable enough to be uninhibited and relaxed in front of the camera. This also helps the model to feel open to trying new and unusual things, which is what can often lead to the best fashion photographs.

A photographer in search of a job should compile a portfolio of his or her best work, which should be taken along everywhere he or she goes. Sometimes opportunity knocks on the strangest doors. One young photographer happened to have her portfolio with her in the rest room at a club, where she met an editor from a style magazine! The editor liked her work and asked her to come in for an interview.

Networking is essential to find a fashion photography job. Talk to anyone you can find who works in any area of fashion, and try to ask him or her for other names and phone numbers. Word-of-mouth is how the best jobs are found. A good place to start is the National Press Photographers Association (NPPA). This is an organization for photojournalists of all kinds. NPPA sponsors workshops and educational events that important people in the industry often attend. NPPA also has an excellent Web site that contains essential career information. Be sure to check out NPPA's magazine, *News Photographer*.

A common job search strategy is to send out résumés, cover letters, and photo samples to magazines and publishing companies. Some photographers decide to open their own studio, which requires some education and/or experience in running a business. Added responsibilities of running a studio include writing contracts, keeping financial records, hiring models and personnel, dealing with permission and copyright issues, and pricing photos.

Average earnings for full-time photographers are around $22,000 yearly. Photographers with experience can earn up to $50,000 and sometimes more. Most self-employed photographers earn less than those on salary, depending on how successful their studios become and how skilled they are at self-promotion. It is also valuable for any photographer to keep up with the latest technology, including digital cameras and computer processing and editing.

What It's Really Like: An Interview with a Fashion Photographer

Joanna is a young freelance photographer who lives in Pittsburgh, Pennsylvania. She has accomplished a great deal in the amount of time she has been taking photographs, including earning money in advertising photography. She also displays her work in gallery shows.

What is your ultimate goal in photography?
My ultimate goal is to shoot for *Vogue* and *Harper's Bazaar* so that I can work with the best people in the business. After that, I would

like to return to Pittsburgh to start up a fashion magazine or agency of some sort. Pittsburgh is in dire need of some fashion inspiration!

What do you like most about photography?
The best thing about fashion photography is getting paid for utilizing your own creativity and having a great deal of fun in the process. It really does not feel like work, at least not to me. I also enjoy the continuous variation in my schedule, meeting new people all the time, and the fact that there is always room for improvement. This provides an element of challenge.

What kinds of problems have you had with clients?
Many insist upon dictating exactly what they want without taking the photographer's style into consideration and without having any real understanding of the photographic process. In many cases, exercising diplomacy has proven useful to me in dissuading a client from a bad or outdated idea. Clients sometimes do not realize that a photographer is not a magician who can make a fifty-five-year-old man look just like Brad Pitt!

A good client allows a photographer to be an important part of the art direction and production process. I have worked with clients who have demanded that I shoot in a certain location, but they have no idea what technical difficulties arise when working in such an environment.

Some clients also have a tendency to choose extremely bad models without consulting me on their choices. Models who do not have professional experience often falter the instant they set foot in front of a camera lens! I have worked with models whose body types are not really suited to modeling as well as some with personalities that were extremely difficult to deal with, even off-camera. Unfortunately, certain models do display behavior that lives up to the "princess" stereotype, throwing tantrums and showing themselves to be immature and conceited. Of course, not all models behave this way.

What are some other challenges you have encountered?
Equipment can be a problem because it is expensive but necessary. Constantly upgrading your equipment does indeed improve the quality of the photos, and it is important in evolving your style. It is also good to get into the habit of bringing backup equipment for important shoots like weddings, which are impossible to reshoot if something goes wrong. Bring extra film, batteries, lights, and bulbs. And always bring duct tape. You would be amazed at how often it has saved the day!

Is it difficult to find clients as a freelancer?
Finding clients can be very taxing work, and its difficulty varies regionally. My experiences in

Pittsburgh have shown me that something like an established "boys' club" network exists, making it difficult for a female photographer to find clients. If you are young, and especially if you are female, it is extremely important to look mature, professional, and confident when presenting yourself to potential employers. Big-budget clients have no time to waste and will tend to become repeat customers if they're satisfied with your work.

A young photographer must also be extremely aggressive and persistent. You could be the best photographer on the planet and still not receive any callbacks. Try not to be too discouraged if the phone does not ring off the hook immediately, although this can seem demoralizing. It is simply part of the process of breaking into fashion photography. One photographer I know, who happens to be very good, sent his portfolio to *VIBE* magazine ten times before he received a callback. Creative self-promotion is essential. And finally, to avoid losing money and friends, remember that payment and agreements should always be made prior to any services rendered.

Do you prefer fashion photography to other kinds? Why?

Yes, I do, because I think it is the ultimate way to create an image. I would rather do that than just shoot what already exists. It is definitely the most fun and artistic kind of photography. I also prefer it because there are not necessarily any technical rules that must be strictly followed, unlike other kinds of photography, which necessitate a specific look or quality.

What are your biggest concerns about your future in this career?

My biggest concern is wondering how long I'll be able to sustain a career in this field. Freelancing has some wonderful advantages, but the business of fashion is very fickle. There always seems to be some sense of insecurity hovering above. For example, two consecutive well-paying months is not a green light to go on a spending spree. It is true when they say that you are only as good as your last photograph.

Are you happy with the pay you have received for your work?

There is always a bit of a dilemma over how much money a shoot is worth. You may have to sacrifice immediate payment in order to secure future work. Overall, I must say I am unhappy with the pay I have received. But different markets have different budgets. The Pittsburgh market, which is where I have been working, generally does not realize the worth of photography and will often settle for substandard work in order to save a few bucks. I try to see it as paying my dues, gaining valuable experience, and building my portfolio.

What prepared you for what you are doing now?

The only photography class I have ever taken was B/W 1 [an introductory course in black-and-white photography] during my sophomore year of high school. Needless to say, I attained only the most rudimentary knowledge of photography through school.

In the summer of 1993, by fluke, I began an internship with a well-known local commercial photographer. There I learned some more darkroom techniques and gained some idea of how the business runs. Mostly my duties included picking up lunch, cleaning out the cluttered basement, and assisting the receptionist. After about three months, I decided to leave, as I felt that I would be able to learn more on my own. And it seemed to work. Nothing is more effective than trial and error. There was a lot of error, and there still is to some degree.

I became a member of Pittsburgh Filmmakers, an organization for the media arts that is complete with all the facilities for photography, filmmaking, and video. There, artists are encouraged to experiment and communicate with other members. So not only was I learning hands-on techniques, but I was also able to view other peoples' work and to ask questions.

What advice would you give someone interested in getting into fashion photography?
I would advise the aspiring young photographer to consistently keep up-to-date, because if you don't, no reputable agency or magazine will give you the time of day. One easy way to stay current is to study various fashion magazines. Look at the lighting, composition, type of film used, location, makeup, styling, the model, and whatever else you can pick up on.

Young photographers also have to think about where they want to live in relation to the kind of photography they are interested in. For example, making money shooting fashion in a small city is pretty much an impossibility. If one is content shooting conservative hair ads or department store ads, shooting in a midsized city like Pittsburgh may actually be a good option. But if someone is intent on revolutionary, edgy, fresh photos for magazines, moving to one of the five fashion centers (New York, London, Milan, Paris, and Los Angeles) will probably be necessary. Once your portfolio is compiled, go to a major fashion mecca and spend as much time there as possible test-shooting some models from the agencies. This is an excellent preliminary technical and social test. If your portfolio is reviewed and accepted, and you are able to produce images that the agent or booker likes, I say continue the rat race!

You must also carefully consider what the client wants to see. For example, *Detour* magazine will not really be interested in viewing catalog tearsheets. However, do show work that you believe in, even if the subject matter is not widely accepted or understood.

It is also a good idea to stake out good hair, wardrobe, and makeup artists who share your vision, and use them often. The final image is a cooperative process. If the photos are technically good but the hair and makeup is outdated or simply bad, then you are wasting your time. If you cannot find anyone to work with your ideas, then try to learn how to do it yourself. There will inevitably be a time when some key person, for whatever reason, does not show up for a shoot.

Who's Who in Fashion

A good way to gain an understanding of the fashion career ladder is to learn about the rungs that others have chosen to climb. In this chapter, we will look at some of the most important and successful people in the fashion world, past and present, and find out how these essential fashion figures achieved what they did. Of course, these are the people in some of the most high-profile positions: fashion and costume designers, fashion photographers, fashion illustrators, and fashion journalists. This is not to say that those who have pursued other careers in fashion are any less important than the ones discussed here. They simply do not generally receive media attention, making their stories less accessible to the world.

Great Designers of the Past

Cristobal Balenciaga

Balenciaga is considered by many to be the greatest fashion designer of all time. What made him special was that his clothes were known for being comfortable, yet incredibly chic and elegant. Women who did not possess the perfect figure of the fashion model could wear his designs because the clothing was crafted so brilliantly. He was also known for seeing many of his projects through entirely on his own, from design right down to sewing, something that few designers today will attempt.

Balenciaga followed a relatively straightforward fashion career path. He was born in 1895 to a Spanish seamstress and became a tailor at a relatively young age. He was encouraged to study design by the Marquesa de Casa Torres, who became his wealthy mentor and sponsor. She supported him when he opened a shop of his own in Spain. He later set up shop in Paris, and in time came to be considered one of the most important and innovative designers of Paris couture.

Balenciaga was also one of the first fashion designers to be commonly referred to as an artist. He studied art, and the influence of some of his favorite artists could be seen in his designs. His work throughout the 1950s and 1960s continues to inspire and influence contemporary designers. He is frequently honored by both art and fashion museums, and he will go down in history for his stunningly beautiful contributions to the world of fashion as well as to the world at large. Balenciaga's career illustrates a path commonly taken by designers and shows the kind of success that can be achieved along the way.

Christian Dior

Christian Dior, a major figure in fashion history, had a true rags-to-riches career. Born into a well-to-do French family in 1905, Dior was completely devastated by the Great

Depression, which began in the late 1920s. He spent much of the next decade in poverty, creating and selling design sketches and fashion illustrations as a means of support. By the late 1930s, his designs had become moderately successful, and Robert Piguet hired him as a designer. In 1941 he began working for another designer, Lucien Lelong, and by 1946 he was able to open his own house with some backing from a French financier.

On his own, Dior's most well-known accomplishment was his "New Look" collection of 1947, which included large, spreading skirts; small waists; and rounded shoulders, a silhouette he continued to develop successfully throughout the 1950s. Christian Dior's legacy to the world of fashion has been rich and enduring and is an inspiration to anyone striving to rise above difficult circumstances.

Gabrielle "Coco" Chanel

Chanel is another one of the most essential names in fashion history. Considered by many to be the single most important female clothing designer, Gabrielle "Coco" Chanel made waves and set standards throughout the '20s and '30s, then again in the late '50s and '60s. Her greatest achievement is the invention of the "little black dress," a fashion staple that remains in every woman's wardrobe decade after decade.

Chanel was born in France in 1883. She began making hats in 1910, and in 1914 she opened her own clothing shop, where she sold her designs. Her styles quickly caught on, and by 1919, after World War I, she was well known in fashion circles. Some of her success was no doubt due to the company she kept, which included famous artists, dancers, and politicians. Making the right friends never hurt anyone's career!

Chanel also had an excellent instinct for knowing what women wanted, and throughout her career she remained faithful to the same basic qualities in her designs. She kept them simple, wearable, and elegant, even when the style of the day called for something different. Chanel's company also branched into jewelry, textile design, and perfume, where her famous Chanel No. 5 became a huge success. The Chanel Company continued to flourish after her death. Today Karl Lagerfeld works as its head designer. Chanel's story emphasizes the importance of instinct, taste, and networking.

Halston (Roy Halston Frowick)

Many people think of Halston only as one of the top American designers of the 1970s, but he was also an extremely successful milliner (hat designer) in the 1960s. It was Halston who designed First Lady Jacqueline Kennedy's trademark pillbox hat, which she wore to her husband's presidential inauguration.

Halston was educated at Indiana University and the Chicago Art Institute; during this time, he began designing and selling hats. In 1959 he began working for Bergdorf Goodman, and his clientele and reputation grew quickly. By the late 1960s, his focus had shifted from hats to ready-to-wear clothing. Halston also designed costumes for dance, notably for the Martha Graham Dance Company.

Halston's designs became extremely popular in the 1970s. His style was simple and classic, and today he is remembered for many original and influential fashion ideas.

Emilio Pucci

If you've seen reruns of the 1960s television sitcom *Bewitched* or videos by the dance band Deee-Lite in the early 1990s, you have probably seen prints designed by Emilio Pucci. Pucci was a designer known for brightly colored, psychedelic dresses, bodysuits, and swimsuits that were popular in the 1960s and were lovingly revived thirty years later.

Pucci did not intend to become a designer or even to work in fashion. He was born an Italian aristocrat and became a member of his country's Olympic ski team in 1933. During World War II, he was an officer in the Italian air force. A fashion photographer in Switzerland noticed the form-fitting, brightly colored ski clothes he was wearing, which Pucci had created for himself. When the pictures attracted favorable attention in the fashion world, he decided to start designing professionally. Soon his prints became high-fashion favorites and were copied in other price ranges as well. Eventually Pucci expanded into accessories, fragrances, sheets, and rugs, among other items.

Gianni Versace

Gianni Versace's name was in the news frequently during the summer of 1997, when he was murdered by Andrew Cunanan, a killer on a murder spree. It was not only the fashion world that mourned publicly for Versace. Musicians, artists, and people from many walks of life expressed their sorrow for the loss of someone who brought a great deal of beauty to the world.

Versace had experience in several different fashion jobs by the time he settled into apparel design. He began his career working as a buyer for his mother's design company in the late 1960s, then moved to Milan, where he studied textiles. In Milan he also worked designing fabrics and clothing for several different companies. Finally, in 1979, he showed his first collection under the name Versace.

From that point on, Versace's popularity exploded as he developed a signature style that blended outrageous glamour with elegance and sophistication, pulling it off with great commercial success and critical acclaim. Versace also tried his hand at costume design and created dazzling ensembles for several popular ballets. Versace's life and influence show how deeply the art of fashion can touch the world. Today his younger sister, Donatella Versace, keeps his unique spirit and style alive as the designer for the house of Versace.

Today's Top Designers

Karl Lagerfeld

Karl Lagerfeld's greatest accomplishment has been bringing the house of Chanel into the modern age. Born in 1939 to German and Swedish parents, Lagerfeld decided at age fourteen to become a fashion designer. Within a year, he was designing for a well-known design house and even winning awards for his work.

Lagerfeld worked for several design houses, spending twenty-one years designing for a company called Chloe. He began working for Chanel while still at Chloe, eventually leaving to devote himself full-time to Chanel and to start a collection under his own name. Throughout his career, he has learned to design many types of items, including gloves, shoes, and furs. His designs are known for being both outrageous and wearable. He uses shock value, when appropriate, to generate excitement for Chanel without ever straying too far from Chanel's original ideals. Lagerfeld is an example of success through determination and hard work.

Giorgio Armani

The name Armani has become synonymous with well-constructed, stylish, and tasteful suits for both men and women. Although the famous apparel designer Giorgio Armani enjoys an impeccable reputation in the fashion world, he has not always been interested in fashion.

In fact, when Armani was young, he planned to work in medicine. Then he tried photography. After deciding that neither career was for him, he began working as an assistant buyer at a men's clothing store in Italy, where he was born. He worked in this position for seven years, all the while learning about clothing and the fashion industry. He then became a fashion designer and worked for ten years with a large manufacturing firm. During this time he gathered even more essential information about designing clothing and surviving in the fashion industry.

Finally, in 1974, Armani put all of his knowledge and experience to work for himself and began designing under his own label. He designed menswear, then moved into women's wear about a year later. His focus was on excellent tailoring and fabrics; neutral colors like beige, black, and gray; and comfortable but elegant shapes.

Today Armani continues that tradition. His importance in fashion is due to consistency in his products, in both quality and style. He and his company have moved with the times, offering the younger and more inexpensive Emporio Armani and A/X labels. Armani's success shows the importance of establishing a reputation through consistent, quality work.

Calvin Klein

Since graduating from New York's Fashion Institute of Technology in 1962, designer Calvin Klein has built a fashion empire. How did he do it? His career path has actually been as simple and straightforward as his designs, yet like his clothes, it has not been completely without risks or variation.

After graduating, Klein worked as a designer's apprentice at several firms. He worked his way up to designer, then in 1968 went into business with a friend to form Calvin Klein Ltd. There Klein continued to develop his signature style, which has been described as spare and understated yet luxurious. He works mostly with neutral colors. Klein has never limited himself to one specific type of clothing, constantly expanding his line to include both women's and men's apparel, blue jeans, shoes, cosmetics, and fragrances.

Like most designers, Klein's reputation grew through consistency, quality, and a healthy dose of scandal and spectacle. In the 1970s his risqué advertising campaigns raised eyebrows and drew attention to his products. This strategy has continued to work for Klein to the present day. Today he is associated with both mature sophistication and youthful hipness, an important duality for a modern designer to achieve. This is best exemplified by his inexpensive ready-to-wear line called CK, which continues to grow in popularity among young people.

Dolce & Gabbana

Two of the most popular designers today are Italians Domenico Dolce and Stefano Gabbana. Known to many young people for their new casual, affordable line of clothing called D & G, Dolce and Gabbana design clothes that are both modern and romantic. Dolce became acquainted with fashion and apparel design through his father's clothing factory as well as by attending fashion school. Gabbana's background was in advertising.

The two met in 1980 when a designer in Milan hired them as assistants. They began working on their own line of clothing after two years. Soon their collections began to receive international attention, and the duo has been growing in popularity ever since. Today they are successful in both men's and women's apparel. Dolce & Gabbana's story is one of great success through the chemistry of collaboration.

John Galliano

If one contemporary designer of the 1990s can be indisputably referred to as an artist, it is John Galliano. It is rare for any designer to be compared to legends such as Chanel and Balenciaga, but Galliano is a trailblazer who has achieved that status in the fashion world at an extraordinarily young age. His creations are stunningly beautiful and complex, drawing on the past yet remaining completely modern.

Galliano was born in 1960. He became interested in studying art at a relatively young age, but his parents would not allow him to pursue this interest until he went to college. His teenage years were difficult as he was often bullied and beaten for being different from his classmates. When he was old enough, he entered one of the most prestigious fashion schools in the world, St. Martin's School of Art in London.

When he began his fashion education, Galliano focused mainly on fabrics. He learned all he could about textiles, including the way their colors worked together and the way that materials draped. He then focused his attention on classes in design. He also enjoyed the booming fashion-inspired nightclub scene in early 1980s London, but not to the extent that many of his classmates did. Often they would spend two days getting their outfits ready for the weekend!

While in school, Galliano developed vital skills working as a dresser at the National Theatre. There he polished shoes, opened doors on cue, and pressed costumes. He also observed the way the actresses wore clothing, and his imagination was constantly stimulated by the productions. "Theatrical flair" is a term often used to describe Galliano's acclaimed work today.

When he had to design an entire collection as his final-year project, Galliano decided to base it on a group of French revolutionaries. It combined all the things he had learned in school, at the theatre, and in the club scene. Today Galliano is still known for creating fresh new designs inspired by specific historical periods.

Galliano's final project attracted media attention and helped him make valuable contacts. He began taking small jobs for little or no money and delved deeper into the London nightclub scene. At the time, clubs were at their peak as dens of creativity and excitement, and Galliano was a well-known part of that energy. He soon found someone to back him financially, then opened a shop that was quite successful.

By 1990 Galliano was participating in Paris ready-to-wear shows. He succeeded Hubert de Givenchy as head designer for the prestigious house of Givenchy in 1995, and by 1997 he had been named chief designer for the house of Dior. There he has continued to develop his themes of theatricality, revolution, and romance.

Betsey Johnson

Betsey Johnson is a unique and truly individual designer. One of her most unusual creations was a clear vinyl dress that came with numbers, stars, and fish that could be pasted on. Johnson is known for designs that are unique, imaginative, and fun to wear.

Johnson's career began when she was taken on as guest editor for *Mademoiselle* magazine during her senior year at Syracuse University. There she made sweaters for all of the editors and as a result landed a job designing for a boutique called Paraphernalia. Though she was only twenty-two at the time, her quirky creations quickly made her an important figure in 1960s' fashion. Betsey Johnson and her designs became associated with youth and the antiestablishment spirit of the times.

Eventually, Johnson and a few friends started their own hip New York boutique called Betsey, Bunky and Nini. By 1978, Johnson was ready to incorporate, and she formed Betsey Johnson, Inc. Her company specializes in dresses and sportswear that hug the body's contours as well as bathing and body suits. Through the 1990s, Betsey Johnson has maintained the spirit of excitement, rebellion, and frivolity that propelled her to the top thirty years earlier.

Todd Oldham

One of today's hippest young designers is Todd Oldham. His clothes are fun yet wearable, and everyone from pop stars to fashion moguls can be seen regularly sporting Oldham originals. He has used unusual materials such as pot holders and sequined horses as part of his creations, and he has received much acclaim for lightening up the often overly serious world of haute couture.

It is interesting to note that Oldham has risen to the top of the fashion heap with no formal education other than a high school degree. He believes that fashion schools can be helpful but that they are unnecessary if you have what it takes. And what it takes, he believes, is innate creativity, vision, and an ability to maintain strength and determination in the face of rejection.

When he was just nine years old, Todd's mother and grandmother taught him to sew. His first job was doing alterations at a Ralph Lauren store. Today he considers that job valuable experience as he was constantly taking apart expensive designer clothes, making changes, and putting them back together again.

Oldham learned to design through trial and error, and by his late teens, he was taking samples of his work around to department stores. The stores liked his ideas, and soon he and his mother were sewing clothes to fill orders for shops like Bloomingdale's, Barney's, and Saks Fifth Avenue. In about five years, Oldham built a reputation. A Japanese company sought him out, wanting to back a new American designer; he seized the opportunity to start his own label.

Today Oldham still remembers and appreciates his roots. His factory is in his hometown in Texas, and his mother and grandmother work for his company. He also likes to promote from within the company, often looking to his receptionists and retail sales staff when a new position opens up. And when he does hire, style and intuition take precedence over schooling and experience. As he has said, creativity cannot be taught.

Costume Designers

Edith Head

Edith Head designed costumes for extremely successful films from the 1930s to the 1970s. Head is an example of someone who was schooled and experienced in a completely different field before landing in fashion. In college she majored in languages, and she went on to teach French.

While still working as a teacher, Head took art classes at night. In the 1920s, she responded to a want-ad seeking an artist for Paramount Pictures. Head then became the assistant to the chief clothing designer at Paramount, and eventually she worked her way up to head designer. She gained experience designing costumes for many different types of films, including musicals, westerns, and even science fiction.

It is interesting to note that Edith Head was never known for a particular signature style. As a costume designer, she had to create whatever clothing was necessary to fit the period and characters for the picture she was working on at the time, and she designed for a diverse range of films. Throughout her illustrious career, Head won a total of eight Academy Awards. Edith Head's career shows that being open to the unplanned and unexpected can lead to unique and satisfying opportunities.

Adrian

Adrian was one of the greatest Hollywood costume designers of the 1920s and 1930s. He also designed made-to-order clothing as well as ready-to-wear. Toward the end of his career, he painted landscapes. Adrian's career is a good example of the importance of networking.

Born Gilbert Adrian, he began studying art and fashion at the School of Fine and Applied Arts in New York in 1921. He remained there for about a year, then left to study in Paris. There he was fortunate enough to meet the theatrical composer Irving Berlin, forming a relationship that turned out to be an excellent connection to the world of costume design. Adrian began designing for musical revues, and by 1923 he was ready for Hollywood.

Another important relationship that Adrian established was with Natasha Rombova, the wife of screen heartthrob Rudolph Valentino. She wanted him to design Valentino's costumes. This association paved Adrian's way to a job with Metro-Goldwyn-Mayer, where he worked as chief designer for fourteen years and designed larger-than-life outfits for legendary stars like Joan Crawford and Greta Garbo.

In 1941, Adrian began designing couture and ready-to-wear clothing under the name Adrian Ltd. He designed for both women and men and even dabbled in perfumes. Adrian eventually decided to retire to Brazil to focus on his painting, but he continued designing costumes until the time of his death.

Fashion Photographers

Richard Avedon

Richard Avedon's career in fashion photography began in 1945 when he was hired as a staff photographer for *Harper's Bazaar* magazine. He came in contact with the magazine through a photography class he had taken, which was taught by *Harper's Bazaar*'s art director. Prior to that he learned photography skills in the merchant marines.

After working with *Harper's Bazaar* for twenty years, Avedon moved on to *Vogue* in 1966. His work is often praised for capturing the spirit of the 1960s. While working as a fashion photographer, Avedon also performed nonfashion work on a freelance basis for other publications. Some of his other projects included visual consulting for films and television as well as the creation of photo collages.

After leaving *Vogue* in 1990, Avedon was hired as staff photographer by *New Yorker* magazine, where his work drifted farther away from fashion and glamour and closer to gritty realism. Much of his fashion and nonfashion work is displayed and celebrated by some of the world's most prestigious art museums.

Bill Cunningham

Bill Cunningham differs from many other fashion photographers in that he is not interested in recording posed glamour and perfection with his photos. He is best known for photographing fashion worn on the street by real people rather than professional models.

Cunningham writes and takes photographs for columns and features for the *New York Times*.

He got his start in the world of fashion working part-time after school at a department store called Bonwit Teller, in Boston. After graduating, Cunningham moved to New York City and was hired by the Bonwit's store there. He also designed and created ladies' masks and headdresses and eventually opened his own hat shop.

Cunningham's career had to be put on hold for a brief period when he was drafted into the army. Once out, he turned his attention from millinery to fashion journalism, writing columns for *Women's Wear Daily* and the *Chicago Tribune*. He began taking photos to illustrate his writing and found that he had a genuine natural talent for photography. In 1993, Cunningham began full-time work at the *New York Times*, where he continues to work today. Bill Cunningham's career is a good example of the infinite paths that one can take in fashion and of the possibilities for crossing over into different areas within the field.

Fashion Illustrators

Antonio

Antonio Lopez (known simply as Antonio) was born in Puerto Rico in 1943. His mother was a dressmaker, and Antonio would sketch dresses for her even in his early childhood. He was fortunate enough to attend the High School of Industrial Art, receiving an earlier start on his artistic education than most young people are able. Antonio followed up at the Fashion Institute of

Technology, and by the time he was nineteen years old, he was working for the respected fashion publication *Women's Wear Daily*.

Antonio's illustrations were often on the cutting edge of whatever art movement was up-and-coming at the time, from pop art to surrealism. He illustrated men's, women's, and children's fashion for *Elle*, American and British *Vogue*, *Harper's Bazaar*, *Interview*, and others. Later in his career, he began teaching illustration in the United States and the Dominican Republic.

Fashion Journalists

Carmel Snow

With a fashionable name like Carmel Snow, into what other industry could this woman have gone? Actually, Snow was born into fashion. Her mother founded a successful dressmaking company called Fox & Co. This led to important connections that helped Snow land an entry-level job at *Vogue*, and by 1929 she had worked her way up to editor.

After three years, Snow took a job with *Vogue*'s number-one competitor, *Harper's Bazaar*. She began there as fashion editor, then became editor, and finally in 1957 moved up to chair of the editorial board. Designers adored her for her style and personality as well as for her remarkable foresight and recognition of talent. Carmel was loyal and worked hard to promote the designers she felt deserved success, and in return they worked hard to please her.

Carmel Snow knew where she belonged early in life, and she was fortunate to be born with important connections and a fabulous name. But she never would have been successful had she not worked to maintain those connections and forge new ones.

Diana Vreeland

Known to many as one of the most colorful and beloved figures in fashion history, Diana Vreeland worked as an editor for both *Harper's Bazaar* and *Vogue*. Later on in her career, she became a museum consultant. One of her most popular quotes is "If you want the girl next door, go next door!" Vreeland's sharp wit was as striking as her look, which she achieved in part using jet-black hair dye and unfathomable amounts of Kabuki-style rouge. As a child she felt ugly, but with humor and style, Vreeland transformed herself into a successful, genuine original.

Vreeland began at *Harper's Bazaar* in 1937 with a whimsical column called "Why Don't You . . ." Within six months she had worked her way up to the position of fashion editor. She remained there for the next twenty-five years and is credited with helping to make *Harper's* one of the world's most popular and influential fashion magazines. She began working for *Vogue* in 1962 as associate editor and was soon promoted to editor in chief. Nine years later, while still working at *Vogue*, she also began consulting at the Costume Institute of the Metropolitan Museum of Art in New York City for special exhibitions. Her work there was instrumental in increasing the recognition of fashion as a valid art form.

Getting a Start

Whatever fashion career you decide on, getting started is always a challenge. You can see from some of the examples in chapter 6 that a career liftoff does not always go smoothly, and some of the greatest successes are completely unplanned. The best you can do is to be as prepared as possible for the unexpected. You may try out five different paths before finding the one that clicks, but if you persevere, success could be right around the corner. Or you may set your sights on one career and follow a straight line to the top. Either way, here are some suggestions for taking your first steps.

Your Portfolio

One of the first things you may need to do when trying to land a fashion job is assemble your portfolio. This is not required for all fashion careers, only the ones related to art and design. If you are going after a career in fashion or textile design, photography, modeling, makeup artistry, or window display design, a striking portfolio of your work is a must. Fashion writers should also have a portfolio of writing samples at their fingertips.

Your portfolio is your ultimate self-promotion tool. This is how you show prospective employers all of the wonderful, creative, and impressive things you know you are capable of doing. It is important that this book not only contain ten to twelve samples of your best possible work but that it be stylish and attention-grabbing as well. Think of it as a flashy advertisement for your skills, one that you can carry around with you at all times. Opportunity knocks at strange times and in unexpected places, and you need to be prepared to answer the door in style.

An employer will evaluate your potential largely based upon the work you show in your portfolio. It speaks volumes about you in a much more efficient manner than any interview ever could. It shows your natural skill and ability as well as what you have learned in fashion school, if you attended one. It also demonstrates your fashion sense, your ideas about personal style, your feel for color and texture, and your ability to conceptualize and coordinate. An employer will most likely determine at a glance if you can be of any use to the company. He or she probably has more drawings and designs to review than is even possible, so don't be boring. Do not include too much of your work; make certain that what you do select is only the absolute best of the best.

Of the work that you do include, try to show the full range of your abilities. For example, if one of your strengths as a photographer is that you can take shadowy black-and-white photographs as well as bright, colorful ones, be sure to include examples of each. Or if you are a model, choose photos that express the different aspects of your personality that come across best on camera, from silly to seductive.

Being able to work in a range of styles and moods is a definite strength in fashion, and versatility is highly valued.

Another strength is foresight. Employers want to be assured that you are not only up on current trends but that you also possess the ability to predict what will be going on two seasons from now. Some people have that natural ability, whereas others successfully cultivate it by studying endlessly the history and cycles of fashion. Either way, this is a trait that can and should be demonstrated skillfully in your portfolio. If you are a budding designer, keep the sketches in your portfolio updated to show what you feel the public will be ready for two seasons from now. If you are a photographer, are your models wearing clothes from three years ago? Models, do your head shots present you sporting outdated hairdos? It will not go unnoticed. In fashion, the original and cutting edge are considered of utmost importance.

One thing an employer will not be looking for is a sloppy worker, so be sure that your portfolio is as neat and organized as possible. This does not mean that you have to go out and spend hundreds of dollars on a fancy portfolio. A simple, inexpensive folder or binder that keeps your work protected and well organized is fine. But smudges, visible mistakes left uncorrected, wrinkled pages, and poor mounting of your work is unacceptable. Every page should be the same size, and any smaller sketches or photos should be mounted on pages that are the same size as the larger ones. Employers want a worker who can make a good impression on clients, and the way you present your portfolio is an indication to them of how you will present ideas to their customers.

It is always a good idea to vary your portfolio slightly between interviews, tailoring your work to different employers. For example, if you are interviewing with a design company known to cater to a conservative clientele, the hot pink jumpsuit and purple handbag you sketched last week should probably be left out for this interview. But it may work well at your interview with the hip, young firm you are scheduled to meet with the following week.

Where can you go for help in assembling your portfolio? Art or fashion teachers and school counselors can be helpful, as well as any working artists you can contact who are willing to give you a few minutes and an opinion. Even friends and family who are not artistically inclined can be helpful in offering constructive criticism and unique perspectives.

Finally, remember to sign your name to each piece of artwork in case it is lost or misplaced. And never borrow or steal anybody else's work. Not only is it a crime, but your employer will be disappointed if you are hired and cannot live up to the plagiarized work in your portfolio.

Your Résumé

So you have a knock-'em-dead portfolio that shows just how brilliantly skilled, creative, and cutting-edge your work is. Now how will you show an employer your past experience and education? Interviewers want to see at a glance exactly how you got to be so good at what you do and where you plan to go with it. This is why the résumé is such a useful tool in securing your first fashion job.

A résumé is basically an informative, one-page advertisement for your skills and abilities. Like the portfolio, your résumé gives you an excellent opportunity to accentuate your strengths to an employer. It is where you state concisely your goals in the fashion industry, your education, and any work experience you have. It is also a good place to list any extracurricular activities or hobbies that you feel are worth mentioning to an interviewer, such as working with your school's drama department or sewing club.

The first thing to put on your résumé is relatively easy. Type your name, address, and telephone number neatly and preferably in bold print at the top of the page. It may be centered or in the left-hand corner. You can also add your e-mail address if you have one.

Now begin to think about your goals. On the résumé your primary goal is called your objective, and it is usually the first thing that you should list. A good objective should not only express what you want to do but also indicate how you expect to do it. For example, "To utilize my education, skills, and creativity in an assistant design position with a large manufacturing firm." It is a good idea to make your objective as specific as possible. Do not simply state your goal as "To work in fashion," as this creates the impression that you do not know yourself very well and may not be a stable, consistent worker. You may want to have several objectives prepared in order to suit the type of company you are interviewing with.

Education is listed next, starting with your most recent degree or diploma. Your résumé should include the names of the schools you attended, the dates, and any special scholarships or honors. Be sure to point out any fashion-related courses you took at each school, even if it is only home economics in high school.

The next part of the résumé, work experience, is often the most difficult for young people just breaking into the industry. If you do not have work experience of any kind, do not create fictitious past jobs! Your prospective employers will find out the truth sooner or later. But do be creative. Just about any part-time job you have had can be presented in a way that relates to the job you are seeking. For example, if you worked in a grocery store and are searching for a job in fashion retailing, be sure to highlight your experience dealing with customers. Or if you worked as a part-time salesperson at Contempo Casuals and are looking for a job as a fashion editor, emphasize the fact that you dealt with clothing and learned about fashion by helping customers put together stylish, flattering outfits.

Do not make this section too long; just state your previous duties briefly and succinctly while subtly emphasizing your strengths. And be sure to include any special recognition or outstanding accomplishments you achieved at your job. Most employers are simply impressed that a student was able to hold down a part-time job while maintaining good grades in school. Also describe any volunteer work you may have done for any organization, from the Red Cross to a local church or synagogue. Directly related to fashion or not, this experience is worth mentioning.

Finally, you can top off your résumé with any hobbies, interests, or special skills that help to define you as a person. It is helpful if these can be related to fashion but not necessary. Theater is an excellent activity as are sports, music, computers, and multiple languages. Employers are looking for well-rounded individuals with multifaceted personalities.

It is extremely important that your résumé be neat and flawlessly typed. It should be presented on strong, quality paper with no wrinkles or creases. You can be creative with the style and font to make it uniquely eye-catching, but try not to overdo it. Above all, the résumé needs to be simple and readable. Flashy tricks that make it difficult to read may distract and frustrate an employer, which can only work against you. Look for examples of résumé styles in guidebooks, which you can find at the library or at your school's guidance office.

Take your time with your résumé! This is your advertisement for your skills, so read it as many times as necessary to make sure that there are no grammatical or spelling errors. Have a friend or family member read it as well. Also be sure that you have covered everything relevant to your career objective and that you have presented the material in a way that accentuates your strengths. Information to leave out includes marital status, religion, age, and race. These facts are unimportant, or should be unimportant, to any employer. And finally, always have an extra copy of your résumé on hand at an interview!

Your Cover Letter

Your résumé is impressive and direct, and neatly typed on clean, strong paper. How do you get it to an employer? If you simply drop it into an envelope addressed to a company, your résumé will probably end up in the receptionist's garbage can. The envelope should be addressed to a specific person at the company. Call the company and ask for the name and title of the person responsible for hiring for the position you seek. If you can't get it, address the envelope to the personnel manager.

All résumés must also include cover letters. The cover letter is a brief, simple letter intended to convince the employer to read the enclosed résumé. It should explain which position you are interested in, mention how you heard about the position, and include a sentence or two explaining why you believe that you are qualified for the job. Like the résumé, it should be neatly typed on high-quality paper.

First, type the date near the top of the left-hand side of the page. Then skip a few lines and type your current address and telephone number. A few more lines down, type the name and title of the person you are writing to, followed by the company's name and address. Below that is the greeting: "Dear Mr./Ms. ___" is appropriate.

The body of the letter starts with which position you are applying for and how you heard about it, then continues with a quick summary of your experience relating to the job and why you are interested. Always finish off the letter by thanking the employer for taking the time and politely asking him or her to call you to arrange for an interview. "Sincerely" and "Sincerely yours" are excellent closings, and do not forget to sign the letter! For examples of cover letters, consult your school's library or career counseling office.

The Interview

This is where all of the preparation pays off. Backed up with a strong résumé and portfolio, your last objective is to dazzle the employer in person. If you have put time into carefully assessing your strengths, weaknesses, skills, and objectives, this should not be too difficult to accomplish. And remember, the interview is not just a time for the employer to make a decision based on your qualifications. It is also an opportunity for you to decide if this is really a company you want to work for. The most successful interviews are two-way streets.

Preparing for an interview is like preparing your résumé, in the sense that you need to verbally convey your strengths and downplay your weaknesses. It is vital that you spend time figuring out how you are going to achieve this. Otherwise you may stumble in the interview and create the wrong impression for the employer, who may only be able to see your weaknesses if you present yourself inadequately.

Punctuality is an important aspect of how you present yourself. Lateness creates a horrible first impression that you may not be able to overcome, and the rest of the interview can be affected by this common mistake. So be sure to depart for the interview early. Allow plenty of extra time in case of car trouble, bus or subway lateness, or taxi unavailability. Also, arriving early will give you a chance to relax and gather your thoughts. Also double-check to make sure you have the correct address and time and that you can pronounce the interviewer's name! Write all of this information down and keep it in your pocket.

Researching the employer is essential. Good resources for this are the Internet, school counselors, people working for the company, and, in the case of large firms, your school or public library. If the company manufactures products, like clothing, cosmetics, accessories, or a fashion magazine, familiarize yourself with them. Buy some of them, or if they are too expensive, just look them over at a store. Be sure to take notes on your observations and go over them before the interview. This information will be invaluable during the interview process, and you can impress your potential employer by mentioning or asking questions about specific products that you are interested in.

Another thing to do before the day of the interview is practice talking about your goals and abilities. You can do this by yourself or with a friend or family member. Try to imagine what this employer might ask of you, prepare an answer, and work on expressing it effectively. For example, "Tell me about yourself" is a common opening question. If you are prepared with a thoughtful response in advance, this question gives you an excellent opportunity to highlight your strengths and the freedom to do it comfortably. Try not to give the employer unnecessary information; chances are the head of personnel at Saks Fifth Avenue does not need to know that your cat's name is Mittens. Keep all responses related to that particular company.

Many interviewers will ask why you are interested in their company. If you have done your research, this question should not only be easy to answer but will also give you the opportunity to convey your knowledge about and enthusiasm for the company. Other questions to prepare for include "Why should we hire you?" "What are your long-term career goals?" and "What makes you think you can make it in fashion?" You can find large lists of commonly asked questions at your school library or career office. Just be sure that you know and understand your experience, skills, and goals, and that you can express them verbally.

Nonverbal communication is something else you can work on before the interview. If you do not normally have good posture, work on sitting up straight in your chair and walking across a room gracefully. This affects the way the employer perceives you. Try to imagine interviewing a candidate for an important position of high responsibility, perhaps assistant fashion editor or makeup artist. Now imagine that candidate slumped over in a chair, fidgeting, and looking nervously around the room. This nervous candidate may be competent, but how would you ever know it? Would you feel confident enough to give him or her a chance?

Appearance is important for any job interview, but it is even more essential for a fashion job interview. Good fashion jobs require good fashion sense, and you will display your ideas about style the instant you walk into the interview. This does not mean that you need to go out and buy the latest expensive Armani suit, but if you can afford it, a designer ensemble would make an excellent impression. Also, try to dress conservatively without being stodgy. Do not wear something outrageous, or you will simply look like a fashion victim who does not know how to assemble an appropriate outfit for a specific occasion.

Most important, look neat and well groomed. The most expensive suit will mean nothing if your hair is messy or your fingernails are dirty. Do not take any unnecessary bags or packages with you, but if you must, try to leave them with the receptionist.

During the interview, appear relaxed in spite of your nervousness. This will help put the interviewer at ease—being on the other side of the desk can be intimidating, too! Be friendly and maintain eye contact. These things help to establish trust and present you as a pleasant person to work with. Be honest and positive when explaining your experience and qualifications. And remember, you are there to gain information as well as give it. Listen attentively but do not go so far as to take notes. It is important to employers that job candidates are interested in and enthusiastic about the company, so smile, be positive, and ask questions.

If your first interview goes badly, do not feel discouraged. You will go through many of them before you truly get the hang of it. Try to make mental notes of areas where you have problems and of questions you have trouble answering so that you can prepare answers in case these difficulties arise again. Your confidence will grow with experience.

Salary is a tricky, sensitive issue to approach, even for longtime employees. When is it appropriate to ask about the starting salary for the position? The end of the interview is the best time, if the subject has not yet been addressed. Ask only if the interview has gone well and you are seriously considering the position. You may be told that a rate of pay has not yet been decided, or you may be asked what kind of range you are looking for. Prepare for this question in advance by speaking with a career counselor and looking through want ads in the newspaper. Try to find out what an average starting salary is for the position you are seeking so that you have a reasonable answer to offer.

If the starting offer is low, bear in mind that fashion jobs are often difficult to come by and experience is valuable. An assistant job with a low starting salary can grow into a very lucrative career later on. Do not let a terrific opportunity pass you by. Starting out in this industry is rough, but the potential rewards can make it worthwhile. Be sure to ask about the company's policy on salary review so you have an idea of when your pay may increase if you perform well.

Closing the interview can sometimes be a bit awkward. Do not stand up before the interviewer indicates that he or she is ready to conclude the interview, and when it is over, be sure to thank him or her for taking the time to meet with you. If you are interested in the position, say so, and perhaps mention something about the company that you are particularly impressed with.

Careers in the Fashion Industry

It is a good idea to send a thank-you letter after the interview. It may seem like a small matter, but it can earn you those extra points you need when the employer is evaluating your candidacy.

If you are offered a position and you want it, say yes and be sure to get all the details you can about starting salary, starting date, where to show up, what to wear, and so on. If you need some time to think it over, it is acceptable to request it. Give the employer a specific date by which you will have a definite answer, and stick to it. If you are definitely not interested in the position, decline politely. You may want to work for this company at a later date, and they could remember you.

Do not let rejection get you down. It is a part of any job search, especially in fashion. If you keep trying, learning, and developing your skills, you are bound to succeed. The fashion industry is a tough egg to crack, but hard work and persistence will get you in the door if you truly want to be there. Financially and creatively, the payoff can be tremendous. Whatever you are searching for in fashion, you will find it if you look hard enough and in the right places!

Glossary

apprentice A beginner who works for an accomplished professional in exchange for experience and education.

catalog copywriter A person who writes the text in catalogs that describes and advertises products.

draping A method of testing out fashion design ideas by strategically hanging fabric on a dress form.

facialist license A license required for a makeup artist to do commercial work.

fashion The prevailing style or custom, as in dress or behavior; also, the business of manufacturing and selling clothing.

flat A detailed sketch showing how a garment is constructed.

freelancing Working on many temporary jobs for different clients rather than being employed by only one company or client on a full-time basis.

haute couture The leading establishment of designers who create exquisite, handmade fashions for an exclusive clientele; French for "high sewing" or "elegant sewing."

head shot A photograph in a model's portfolio that shows only the face, neck, shoulders, and hair.

Careers in the Fashion Industry

Industrial Revolution The shift from home-based hand manufacturing to large-scale factory production. It occurred first in the eighteenth century.

jeweler A person who works in jewelry sales, buying, repair, design, manufacturing, or appraisal. A jeweler usually specializes in one of these areas.

knocking off The practice of copying haute couture designs and manufacturing them using less expensive materials.

line (of clothing) A collection of thematically linked clothing created by a designer.

milliner A person who designs and makes hats.

muslin Sturdy, plain, cotton fabric used in the preproduction process of clothing design.

open call A scheduled time when models can show their pictures to an agent.

portfolio A collection of sketches or photographs used to demonstrate the skills of people seeking jobs in many areas of fashion.

power loom A powered apparatus for making thread or yarn into cloth by weaving strands together at right angles.

résumé A one-page, typed advertisement for the qualifications and experience of a potential employee.

textile A cloth or fabric, especially one manufactured by weaving or knitting.

textile chemistry A field of work and study focused on the physics and chemistry of the compounds that form the fibers in textiles.

textile technology The use of modern technology to create fabrics; it includes textile design, textile engineering, textile management technology, and textile chemistry.

trimmer The person who assists a window display designer.

For More Information

Fashion Organizations and Schools

American Apparel and Footwear Association
1601 North Kent Street, Suite 1200
Arlington, VA 22209
(800) 520-2262
Web site: http://www.americanapparel.org

Council of Fashion Designers of America
1412 Broadway
New York, NY 10018
(212) 302-1821

Fashion Institute of Technology
Office of Admissions
Building C, Room 159
Seventh Avenue at 27th Street
New York, NY 10001
(212)760-7675
Web site: http://www.fitnyc.suny.edu

Men's Fashion Associations of America
240 Madison Avenue
New York, NY 10016
(212) 683-5665

Moore College of Art and Design
20th and the Parkway
Philadelphia, PA 19103
(215) 568-4515
Web site: http://www.moore.edu

United Garment Workers of America
4207 Lebanon Road, Suite 200
Hermitage, TN 37076
(615) 889-9221

Journalism Associations

American Society of Magazine Editors
919 Third Avenue, 22nd Floor
New York, NY 10022
(212) 872-3700
Web site: http://asme.magazine.org/about_asme/index.html

American Society of Media Photographers, Inc.
150 North Second Street
Philadelphia, PA 19106
(215) 451-2767
Web site: http://www.asmp.org

National Press Photographers Association
3200 Croasdaile Drive, Suite 306
Durham, NC 27713
(919) 383-7261
Web site: http://www.nppa.org/default.cfm

Organizations for Accessory Design

Gemological Institute of America
Robert Mouawad Campus
5345 Armada Drive
Carlsbad, CA 92008
(800) 421-7250
Web site: http://www.gia.org

Headwear Information Bureau
302 West 12th Street, PH-C
New York, NY 10014
(212) 627-8333
Web site: http://www.hatsny.com/HIB/index.html

Shoe Service Institute of America
Educational Library
5024 Campbell Boulevard, Suite R
Baltimore, MD 21236
(410) 931-8100

Organizations for Sales Representatives
Manufacturers' Agents National Association
P.O. Box 3467
23016 Mill Creek Drive
Laguna Hills, CA 92654
(877) 626-2776
Web site http://www.manaonline.org

Web Sites
Due to the changing nature of Internet links, the Rosen Publishing
Group, Inc., has developed an online list of Web sites related to
the subject of this book. This site is updated regularly. Please use
this link to access the list:

http://www.rosenlinks.com/crl/fain

For Further Reading

Aucoin, Kevyn, and Tina Gaudoin. *The Art of Make-up*. New York: Callaway Editions, 1994.

Hewitt, Sally. *The Clothes We Wear*. Austin, TX: Raintree/Steck-Vaughn, 1997.

Koester, Pat. *Careers in Fashion Retailing*. New York: The Rosen Publishing Group, Inc., 1990.

McConathy, Dale, and Diana Vreeland. *Hollywood Costume: Glamour! Glitter! Romance!* New York: H. N. Abrams, 1976.

McDowell, Colin. *Galliano*. New York: Rizzoli International Publications, 1998.

Milbank, Caroline Reynolds. *New York Fashion: The Evolution of American Style*. New York: Abrams, 1989.

Skrebneski, Victor, and Laura Jacobs. *The Art of Haute Couture*. New York: Abbeville Publishing Group, 1995.

Steele, Valerie. *Fifty Years of Fashion: New Look to Now*. New Haven, CT: Yale University Press, 1997.

Wolfe, Mary Gorgen. *Fashion: A Study of Clothing Design and Selection, Textiles, the Apparel Industries, and Careers*. Tinley Park, IL: Goodheart-Wilcox Co., 1997.

Index

About the Author

John Giacobello is a musician and freelance writer who resides in New York City. Before moving to New York, he wrote fashion-related articles for various newspapers and magazines in Pittsburgh.

Series Design

Danielle Goldblatt

Layout

Geri Giordano